Romanticism and Parenting

Romanticism and Parenting
Image, Instruction and Ideology

Edited by

Carolyn A. Weber

CAMBRIDGE SCHOLARS PUBLISHING

Romanticism and Parenting: Image, Instruction and Ideology, edited by Carolyn A. Weber

This book first published 2007 by

Cambridge Scholars Publishing

15 Angerton Gardens, Newcastle, NE5 2JA, UK

British Library Cataloguing in Publication Data
A catalogue record for this book is available from the British Library

Copyright © 2007 by Carolyn A. Weber and contributors

All rights for this book reserved. No part of this book may be reproduced, stored in a retrieval system, or transmitted, in any form or by any means, electronic, mechanical, photocopying, recording or otherwise, without the prior permission of the copyright owner.
ISBN 1-84718-295-X; ISBN 13: 9781847182951

*For my mother, Ann M. Drake,
who, by enduring example,
gave me a deep love of reading
and an even deeper love of parenting.*

- C.A.W.

TABLE OF CONTENTS

Acknowledgments ix

List of Illustrations xi

Introduction 1
Carolyn A. Weber, Seattle University

Chapter One 7
Tipu Sultan's Sons and Images of Paternalism in Late
Eighteenth-Century Romantic British Art
Catherine E. Anderson, Brown University

Chapter Two 29
Richard Edgeworth as Parent and Educator
Brian Hollingworth, University of Derby

Chapter Three 37
Saving Mrs. Mason's Soul: How Blake Rewrites Mary Wollstonecraft's
Original Stories from Real Life
Amy Carol Reeves, University of South Carolina

Chapter Four 53
Matrilineal Descent: Mother, Daughter, and the Seeking Soul in Mary
Shelley's *Proserpine*
Carolyn A. Weber, Seattle University

Chapter Five 74
Family Systems Theory and "The Man of Fifty Years" in Goethe's
Wilhelm Meister's Journeyman Years
Ingrid Broszeit-Rieger, Oakland University

Chapter Six 87
Wordsworth's Mother Tongue: Mourning, Language and Identity
in "The Emigrant Mother"
Robert C. Hale, Monmouth College

Chapter Seven 103
Reforming the Space of the Child: Infancy and the Reception of
Wordsworth's "Ode"
David B. Ruderman, University of Michigan

Chapter Eight 128
The Founding Father: Benjamin Franklin and his Autobiography
Jeff Morgan, Lynn University

Chapter Nine 138
On Romanticism and Parenting in Practise
Sarah Moss, University of Kent at Canterbury

List of Contributors 146

ACKNOWLEDGMENTS

Romanticism is a longstanding and varied field of study. Parenting, it is safe to say, is perhaps the oldest profession, as a consequence of any act of "creation". What this collection does by bringing these two entities together is, as poet Adrienne Rich writes, "to do something very common in [its] own way." In its study of Romantic complications of the constructions of parenting, this volume makes parenting the centre of academic inquiry. By bringing together such hitherto disparate notions of academics and parenting, the collection opens doors, not only into the field of Romantic studies, but also into how academics themselves conceptualize, and even personally function (or merely attempt to survive) as parents. As the organizer of the Romanticism and Parenting Conference at Seattle University two summers ago that lead to this collection, I can say that I have never experienced a warmer or more collegial group of participants. Symbolically put, the contributors of this volume have become "family": we stay in touch, despite the miles, supporting each other's academic and parenting endeavours, and cherish the time we spent together at the conference and on this project as a memorably intimate experience, not usually found in the rush and anonymity of international conferences. I wish to thank the contributors for their personal investment in this project, for their professionalism, and most all, for their friendship.

That being said, as all families go, this one also has a history and thus a legacy. This collection is the result of much prior vision and effort. As the editor, I speak with a collaborative voice to thank those who organized the two prior Romanticism and Parenting conferences, which inspired the most recent one that took place in Seattle, Washington. The first was organized by Dr. Elizabeth Fay (University of Massachusetts, Boston), and was renown for its cutting edge discussion. Dr. Christopher Rovee (Stanford University) warmly hosted the second, and provided me with much collegial guidance and feedback. Without these early conference organizers' commitment to expanding upon Romantic ideologies of parenting, and the repercussions for academics today, both personally and professionally, our third conference never would have materialised. We modelled the intimate structure of the conference on their previous designs to promote intellectual as well as social community, and for that experience we are particularly grateful.

The contributors wish to thank our many colleagues involved in the tedious but caring peer reviews of our work. For me as editor, many thanks also go out to my support team at Seattle University. When, as a newer faculty member, I first tentatively took my idea to host this conference to my chair, Dr. Edwin Weihe, he responded with his usual magnanimity and enthusiasm. As a result, he nurtured my development not only as a scholar, but as a true academic "host" – a wonderfully enriching experience in a new academic "home". To senior colleague and invaluable mentor, Dr. Mary-Antoinette Smith, also go out heartfelt thanks. She brought a helpful Victorian perspective to our Romantic discussions of the child, and believed in and supported the project from its very genesis. I also wish to thank Drs. Maria Bullón-Fernandez and Nalini Iyer of Women Studies and the Wismer Center at Seattle University for their financial support of the conference, the Dean's office of the College of Arts and Sciences for my summer grant and editorial assistance, the English department, Claire Tarlson for helping to organize panels, and my two work studies: Abby Murphy, who cheerfully trekked conference participants around Seattle, and Patrick Dominguez, who helped painstakingly prepare the entire manuscript for press.

Finally, a special thanks to the inner sanctum. With uncanny albeit appropriate timing, I found out I was pregnant shortly after hosting the conference. Whilst colleagues joked about the event as evidence of how seriously I take my research, I could not have prepared the entire volume without the subsequent loving childcare provided by dear friends Lisa Kissinger and Janel Collier. Little Victoria Kelly Weber has opened my eyes and my heart beyond a love ever previously imaginable, which now informs my work and my priorities with a deeper humanity. In Blake's words, Little Lamb, God bless thee. But my deepest gratitude of all extends to my husband, Kent, whose unconditional love and support light up my life. Kent, you make everything possible. You are the love of my life, and now you wear the crown of "daddy", too – shining, invincible and our hero beyond words. Victoria and I adore you. Thanks for helping mommy use her words.

C. Weber
May 2007

LIST OF ILLUSTRATIONS

Chapter One

Fig. 1. Robert Home, *Lord Cornwallis Receiving Tipu Saib's Sons as Hostages, 1792*, c. 1792-95. London: National Army Museum.

Fig. 2. Henry Singleton, *Departure of the Hostages from Seringapatam*, 1793 (engraved by J. Grozer as *The Sons of Tipu Sultan Leaving their Father*, 1793). Courtesy of the Council of the National Army Museum, London.

Fig. 3. Mather Brown, *Lord Cornwallis Receiving the Sons of Tipu Sultan as Hostages*, c.1793. Anne S. K. Brown Military Collection, John Hay Library, Brown University.

Fig. 4. Anonymous, *Tippoo Saib's Two Sons deliver'd up to Lord Cornwallis*, 1792. Hand-coloured print published by Robert Sayer, 1792. Anne S. K. Brown Military Collection, John Hay Library, Brown University.

Fig. 5. J. John Smart, *Muiz-ud-Deen*, 1794. Graphite. © Copyright The Trustees of the British Museum.

Fig. 6. Henry Singleton, *The Surrender of Two Sons of Tippoo Sultan* (engraved by Anthony Cardon, 1802). Anne S. K. Brown Military Collection, John Hay Library, Brown University.

Fig. 7. Henry Singleton, *The Destruction of the Bastille* (engraved by W. Nutter, 1792). © Copyright The Trustees of the British Museum.

Fig. 8. Thomas Stothard, *The Departure from the Zenana (The Surrender of the Children of Tippoo Sultaun on the Fourth of May 1799)*, colour engraving by James Daniell, 1800. Anne S. K. Brown Military Collection, John Hay Library, Brown University.

Fig. 9. George Morland, *The Slave Trade*, 1788 (mezzotint engraving by John Raphael Smith, 1791). Davison Art Center, Wesleyan University. Photo: R. J. Phil.

Chapter Three

All illustrations from Wollstonecraft's *Original Stories*
Fig. 1. William Blake, Plate 1, 1791. New Haven: Beinecke Rare Book and Manuscript Library, Yale University.
Fig. 2. William Blake, Plate 2, 1791. New Haven: Beinecke Rare Book and Manuscript Library, Yale University.
Fig. 3. William Blake, Plate 3, 1791. New Haven: Beinecke Rare Book and Manuscript Library, Yale University.
Fig. 4. William Blake, Plate 4, 1791. New Haven: Beinecke Rare Book and Manuscript Library, Yale University.
Fig. 5. William Blake, Plate 5, 1791. New Haven: Beinecke Rare Book and Manuscript Library, Yale University.
Fig. 6. William Blake, Plate 6, 1791. New Haven: Beinecke Rare Book and Manuscript Library, Yale University.

INTRODUCTION

CAROLYN A. WEBER, SEATTLE UNIVERSITY

> And thou, my babe, though born, like me, for woman's weary lot,
> Smile – to that wasting of the hearts, my own! I leave thee not;
> Too bright a thing art *thou* to pine in aching love away,
> Thy mother bears thee far, young fawn, from sorrow and decay.
>
> She bears thee to the glorious bowers where none are heard to weep,
> And where th' unkind one hath no power again to trouble sleep;
> And where the soul shall find its youth, as wakening from a dream –
> One moment, and that realm is ours: on, on, dark rolling stream![1]

When we think of Romanticism and the child, we tend to think immediately of William Blake's portrayal of infantine purity subjected to the exploitation of self and world in his collection *Songs of Innocence and Experience*, or of the psychological and spiritual implications of childhood for the adult consciousness, as with William Wordsworth's declaration that "the child is father of the man".[2] In traditional critical discussions of Romanticism, and in the custom of secularizing the spiritual, children become icons: primitivist figures to be celebrated, separated, even venerated because of their evocation of the divine, and because of their inherent criticism of the high rationalism of solely capitalistic, irreverent, scientific, or otherwise put, unimaginative adults. Children bring us back to "ourselves," or, more aptly for the Romantics, back to our original oneness with divinity. Such idealized notions of the child cause us to "re-member:" as daemons of the quotidian, children help us very busy, very accomplished, very cogent and self-important adults see back "into the life of things". They remind us to re-imagine the world by the very fact, so to speak, that imagination, for them, is the most legitimate, if perhaps only, reality.

---

[1] Felicia Dorothea Hemans, "Indian Woman's Death Song," ll. 36-43, *Romantic Women Poets*, Ed. Duncan Wu. Oxford: Blackwell, 1997: 552-53.
[2] "My Heart Leaps Up".

And yet such "romanticised" notions of the child are not, plainly, so unwaveringly "romantic". No surprise, given the slipperiness of the term "Romanticism" itself. Despite the fact, however, that children were being sentimentalized, even transcendentalised, long before Wordsworth and Blake were using them for symbolic fodder, the child does evolve into something distinct and unique under the pen of the Romantics, something more transfixing because of its ambiguities and even inconsistencies. Alan Richardson aptly identifies it as thus: that the Romantics "succeeded at popularizing an image of the child which was no less powerful for being somewhat incoherent, intermingling the sentimentalism of eighteenth-century verse, the transcendentalism of Vaughan, a Lockean emphasis on the child's malleability, and a Rousseauvian faith in original innocence and "natural" principles of growth".[3]

And yet what of the representation of actual *parenting* in Romantic texts? The relationship between children and their parents in Romantic literature still remains critically overlooked at large. Whether in overt or encoded terms, whether between two fictional characters or between an author and his or her own children, the complications of ideological constructions of children by the parents themselves in Romantic discourse beg further discussion. In Felicia Hemans' poem "Indian Woman's Death Song," from which I took the epigraph above, the speaker, a Native American mother betrayed by her lover, tells her infant girl of the promise of escape from their current suffering in the afterlife. The poem is constructed as the mother's justification of her act of suicide (and of infanticide) before their canoe's fatal plunge over the waterfall. These lines offer an appropriate point of departure because of their complex capturing of several themes that will be examined in this volume regarding parent-child relationships as well as constructions of parenting, especially against notions of "audience," whether it be the child him or herself, an intimate coterie or a larger, even more political, readership. The ways in which one constructs oneself as parent find parallels in authorial implications of power as well. Whether "family" involves one parent warning his or her same sex child of the gendered trappings of the world, or an educator attempting to reconcile (or not) theoretics with the pragmatics of procreation, or a politician acting as patriarch to a burgeoning nation, we see that the Romantics show us how parenting assumes an aesthetics of responsibility from a position of empowerment, or at the very least, decodification. The great parent is the great teacher and vice versa; while the poet may help us see things anew, the parent

---

[3] Richardson (1999), pp. 23-43.

helps us navigate life as it is. Writing thereby becomes a form of parenting, not only in its generating of textual progeny, but in its patriarchal or maternal stance (whether conformist or subversive) towards a readership that needs to be "taught" something. The effect is not merely didactic, though certainly ideas or "facts" are conveyed to this end. But rather, as many of the ensuing essays explore, parenting principles, as tied up with desires to particularly bestow moral responsibility, become means by which to claim "legitimate" ways of rejecting or reinstating the "other".

Taken in this light, children of such Romantic discourses are not limited to poetic or iconic symbols, but in fact reflect the appropriation, victimization or, at times, attempted healing of not only their parents, but of those who behold them. Parents teach us how to "read reality:" they help us de-code the world and, in turn, they also form how we encode it. Does this de-coding necessarily lead to a de-mystifying? And does this encoding necessarily lead to the creation of "isms" (racism, classicism, and so forth) that classify our perceptions, and thus, in turn, our actions? In response, the essays of this volume look at how parents create ways of being in the world; they both liberate and implicate as the experienced guides and signifiers of the "innocent", moved by motives as seemingly mutually inclusive, but which prove at times to be interdependent, as love and power.

This collection has its roots in discussions from the 2005 Romanticism and Parenting Conference held at Seattle University in Seattle, Washington. To date, no other single volume exists in the academic market with such a specific focus on Romantic representations of parents and parent-child relations through such a wide spectrum of perspectives. Other works address Romanticism and related themes, such as the family and domesticity, or the cult of the child, although books in this field tend to remain limited to the contexts of specific authors or groups (such as the Godwin/Shelley circle). For instance, Judith Plotz provides a fascinating study of how seemingly enchanting Romantic textual depictions of childhood's beauty and power actually come to betray a darker vision that problematises Romantic childhood joy and idyllic innocence. Plotz's claim that the "embrace of absolute child is both a creative and destructive force", however, remains limited to her study of four Romantics, namely Lamb, Coleridge, Wordsworth and DeQuincey. The other thread dominating existing studies involving the Romantic child privilege theories of education and language, as influenced by philosophers (such as Locke, Rousseau, and Godwin) and proto-child psychology movements, social reform acts or linguistic theories. Important discussions in this field include *Lessons of Romanticism: A Critical Companion*, eds. Thomas Pfau and Robert F. Gleckner (Duke University Press, 1998), *The Educational Legacy of Romanticism*, ed. John Willinsky (Wilfrid Laurier University Press, 1990), and, of course, Alan Richardson's very important *Literature, Education and Romanticism* (Cambridge University, 1995). Substantial discussion exists not only of the development of the child as cultural symbol, but also of parenting, such as depicted in Roger Cox's sweeping study of the child in history, from the "child of Puritanism" through the Englightenment, Romanticism, Victorianism and into the millennium (*Shaping Childhood: Themes of Uncertainty in the History of Adult-Child Relationships*, London and New York: Routledge, 1996). However, such work stems from primarily a sociological platform as opposed to a literary one. No collection as of yet has been dedicated fully to a discussion of parent-child relations, and an analysis of their discourses and aesthetics, in Romantic literature and the arts. Perhaps the closest to achieving this aim thus far are the two very insightful volumes edited by James Holt McGavran, Jr.: *Romanticism and Children's Literature in Nineteenth-Century England* (University of Georgia Press, 1991) and *Literature and the Child: Romantic Continuations, Postmodern Contestations* (University of Iowa Press, 1999). While the focus with both collections remains relatively on the symbolic figure of the child, representations of childhood and the politics of children's reading, they do offer interesting forays into how parenting can assume poetic and even religious instructive paradigms, such as in McGavran's own essay in the former collection "Catechist and Visionary: Watts and Wordsworth in 'We are Seven' and the 'Anecdote for Fathers'". Just this year, Julie Kipp published her exciting study entitled *Romanticism, Maternity and the Body Politic* (Cambridge University, 2007), but its emphasis remains with mothering, as opposed to wider notions of "parenting". Caroline Gonda provides a compelling complementary point of view to parenting in her volume *Reading Daughters' Fictions, 19709 – 1834: Novels and Society from Manley to Edgeworth* (Cambridge University, 2005). But again, prominence is given to feminist discussions and to the "child", or in this case, "daughtership". In general, then, as we can see, new criticism in the area of understanding implications of "Romantic parenting" is needed, as most recent discussions date primarily from the 1980's and 90's. Otherwise, the still fledgling scholarship in the field of Romantic parenting remains limited to single articles in scholarly journals, or focused studies within a range of authors, rather than within a convenient or sustained collection on the topic across many perspectives. Addressing this need in Romantic studies propelled the collection of these essays for the purpose of this book.

This collection acknowledges traditional discussions of such quintessentially "Romantic" themes as the child, education and familial politics while building upon contemporary innovative arguments, such as cognitive and family systems theories. As a result, the essays in *Romanticism and Parenting: Image, Instruction and Ideology* offer a fresh, timely, and cutting edge contribution to the field of Romantic studies. Chapters in the collection range from examining didactic children's literature to complicating constructions of the family politic at personal, communal and nationalistic levels. As its title indicates, the collection addresses parent-child discourses among Romantic writers along three venues: image, instruction and ideology. "Image" pertains to the aesthetics of such discourses, in the semblance and structure of family systems (such as in Ingrid Rieger's essay on Goethe's representation of the family) as well as in actual visual arts (as seen in Catherine Anderson's examination of paternalism in Romantic British art and in Amy Reeves's article on Blake and Wollstenecraft). "Instruction" represents the educational values extended between parent figures and their audience, whether it is the instruction of a nation (as argued in Jeff Morgan's essay on Benjamin Franklin) or of the soul (as seen in Brian Hollingworth's discussion of the Edgeworths). "Ideology" conveys the dynamics of privatized discourses that take on larger political significance (as seen, for example, in the adaptation of myth in my discussion of Mary Shelley's *Proserpine*, or in Robert Hale's study of mourning mothers, or in David Ruderman's examination of the problematically fictionalized "Romantic child"). While challenging and deepening an understanding of Romantic studies, the collection also makes connections to current issues (as exemplified in Sarah Moss's comparison of pregnancy manuals and social dictates, then and now).

We contributors came together in the greatest collegial spirit as academics interested personally and professionally in the politics of parenting. For, as scholars steeped in the politics of production and the attractions and yet ironies of (pro)creation, how can one be a Romanticist without being drawn to the child, and thus, back to the parent? As Richardson writes:

> In its threatened dissolution, childhood brings us up against the limits of certain canonical forms of Romanticism even in registering their cultural force. It may equally, however, raise questions regarding both the limits of a postmodern devaluation of Romantic values and the potential for finding

something to recuperate in a discourse that, as it recedes from us in time, throws our own cultural practices into sharper outline.[4]

Consequently, the collection reveals how the Romantic period has come to profoundly influence our own current constructions of the family and such related terms as maternity, paternity, childhood, the body and "generation" in western culture.

Works Cited

Cox, Roger. *Shaping Childhood: Themes of uncertainty in the history of adult-child relationships*. London and New York: Routledge, 1996.

Felicia Dorothea Hemans, "Indian Woman's Death Song," ll. 36-43, *Romantic Women Poets*, Ed. Duncan Wu. Oxford: Blackwell, 1997: 552-53.

Gonda, Caroline. *Reading Daughters' Fictions, 1709-1834: Novels and Society from Manley to Edgeworth*. Cambridge University Press, 2005.

Kipp, Julie. *Romanticism, Maternity and the Body Politic*. Cambridge University Press, 2007.

McGavran, Jr., James Holt. Ed. *Romanticism and Children's Literature in Nineteenth-Century England*. Athens and London: University of Georgia Press, 1991.

—. Ed. *Literature and the Child: Romantic Continuations, Postmodern Contestations*. Iowa city: University of Iowa Press, 1999.

Pfau, Thomas and Robert F. Gleckner, Eds. *Lessons of Romanticism, A Critical Companion*. Durham and London: Duke University Press, 1998.

Plotz, Judith. *Romanticism and the Vocation of Childhood*. New York: Palgrave, 2001.

Richardson, Alan. *Literature, Education and Romanticism*. Cambridge University Press, 1995.

—. "Romanticism and the End of Childhood." Ed. James Holt McGavran, Jr. *Literature and the Child: Romantic Continuations, Postmodern Contestations*. Iowa city: University of Iowa Press, 1999. 23-43.

Willinsky, John. Ed. *The Educational Legacy of Romanticism*. Waterloo: Wilfrid Laurier University Press, 1990.

---

[4] Richardson (1999), p. 24.

CHAPTER ONE

TIPU SULTAN'S SONS AND IMAGES OF PATERNALISM IN LATE EIGHTEENTH-CENTURY BRITISH ART

CATHERINE E. ANDERSON, BROWN UNIVERSITY

In the spring of 1792, word reached England that Lord Charles Cornwallis, Governor-General of India, had at long last defeated Tipu Sultan, the so-called "Tiger of Mysore." Tipu, king of the southern state of Mysore and Britain's greatest foe in India, had agreed to Cornwallis' terms of surrender, which included the handing over of two of his sons as hostages. This event quickly became the most celebrated aspect in contemporary visual accounts of the victory over Tipu during the Third Mysore War, providing artists with material both propagandistic and sentimental. Cornwallis, assuming the role of the boys' father, demonstrated magnanimity toward the sons of his enemy, thereby inverting captivity narratives such as those of British subjects held prisoner by Tipu. Later, during the Fourth and final Mysore war in 1799, two of the sultan's sons surrendered themselves to General David Baird in an effort to save their family. Baird, like Cornwallis, became another surrogate father to the boys. Visual and literary descriptions of both the hostage-taking and the later surrender center "on the transfer of paternity": as Kate Teltscher has noted, "Cornwallis accepts Tipu's sons as his own in a ceremonial enactment of the British appropriation of the East."[1] Clearly, this is the overriding message that the pictures conveyed. However, I shall demonstrate that a larger narrative emerges once the images are placed in the context of more global events. British anxieties over the French

---

[1] Kate Teltscher, *India Inscribed: European and British Writing on India, 1600-1800* (Delhi: Oxford UP, 1995), 248.

Revolution permeate these Indian subjects through the trope of paternalism, an interpretation made even more compelling by Tipu's own alliances with the French.[2] Additionally, the question remains of how tearing apart one family—removing the boys from their actual father—could be made acceptable in the eyes of the British public, particularly in light of the fact that this era marked the height of the anti-slavery campaigns in England in which abolitionists attacked planters and slave traders for destroying the families of the Africans they enslaved. Here we need to investigate how Tipu was constructed as a bad father—alternately tyrannical or effeminate—and how Cornwallis, and later Baird, were presented as the boys' good and therefore rightful father. By extension, since Tipu was a bad father, he was a bad king, and the British Governor-General or his officers emerge from the narrative as the beneficent and rightful rulers of India.

Cornwallis' encounter with Tipu began when the Mysorean ruler, whose father Haider Ali had also been staunchly resistant to British incursions, attacked the neighboring territory of Travancore in 1789. The Rajah of Travancore sought help from the British, and the East India Company, under Cornwallis, declared war on Tipu. Though British forces advanced towards Tipu's capital of Seringapatam, Tipu cut off their supply lines and forced them to retreat before they were finally able to regroup and attack the capital in 1792. In February of that year, Tipu agreed to the British terms of surrender in the Treaty of Seringapatam, wherein he gave up half of his land and a large sum of money, ending the Third Mysore War.[3] In order to ensure that Tipu would abide by the terms of the treaty, the British kept two of his sons as hostages. When Tipu fulfilled the terms of the treaty in 1794, his sons, who had been kept in Madras, were returned.

The story of Cornwallis' reception of the hostage princes was rapidly disseminated through periodicals and books, and illustrated by several artists in oil paintings and engravings. Major Alexander Dirom's version of the story, published in 1793 and apparently based on an eyewitness account by the artist Robert Home, offers a detailed description of the spectacle at Seringapatam, and merits quoting in length:

---

[2] Linda Colley discusses the significance of the Mysore-France connection in *Captives: The Story of Britain's Pursuit of Empire and How Its Soldiers and Civilians were Held Captive by the Dream of Global Supremacy, 1600-1850* (New York: Pantheon, 2002), 296-7.
[3] The First and Second Mysore Wars had been fought in 1766-69 and 1780-84, respectively, between the British East India Company and Haider Ali.

Tipu Sultan's Sons and Images of Paternalism in Late Eighteenth-Century British Art

On the 26th [of February] about noon, the Princes left the fort, which appeared to be manned as they went out, and every where crouded with people, who, from curiosity or affection, had come to see them depart. The Sultaun himself, was on the rampart above the gateway. They were saluted by the fort on leaving it, and with twenty-one guns from the park as they approached our camp, where the part of the line they passed, was turned out to receive them. The vakeels [Tipu's representatives] conducted them to the tents which had been sent from the fort for their accommodation, and pitched near the mosque redoubt, where they were met by Sir John Kennaway, the Maharatta and Nizam's vakeels, and from thence accompanied by them to head quarters.

The Princes were each mounted on an elephant richly caparisoned, and seated in a silver howder, and were attended by their father's vakeels, and the persons already mentioned, also on elephants. The procession was led by several camel harcarras, and seven standard-bearers, carrying small green flags suspended from rockets, followed by one hundred pikemen, with spears inlaid with silver. Their guard of two hundred Sepoys, and a party of horse, brought up the rear. In this order they approached head quarters, where the battalion of Bengal Sepoys, commanded by Captain Welch, appointed for their guard, formed a street to receive them.

Lord Cornwallis, attended by his staff, and some of the principal officers of the army, met the Princes at the door of his large tent as they dismounted from the elephants; and, after embracing them, led them in, one in each hand, to the tent; the eldest, Abdul Kalick, was about ten, the youngest, Mooza-ud-Deen, about eight years of age. When they were seated on each side of Lord Cornwallis, Gullam Ally, the head vakeel, addressed his lordship as follows. "These children were this morning the sons of the Sultan my master; their situation is now changed, and they must look up to your lordship as their father."

Lord Cornwallis, who had received the boys as if they had been his own sons, anxiously assured the vakeel and the young Princes themselves, that every attention possible would be shewn to them, and the greatest care taken of their persons. Their little faces brightened up; the scene became highly interesting; and not only their attendants, but all the spectators were delighted to see that any fears they might have harboured were removed, and that they would soon be reconciled to their change of situation, and their new friends.

The Princes were dressed in long white muslin gowns, and red turbans. They had several rows of large pearls around their necks, from which was suspended an ornament consisting of a ruby and an emerald of considerable size, surrounded by large brilliants; and in their turbans, each had a sprig of rich pearls. Bred from their infancy with infinite care, and instructed in their manners to imitate the reserve and politeness of age, it astonished all present to see the correctness and propriety of their conduct.[4]

Dirom's description dwells upon the exotic, picturesque aspects of the scene, allowing readers in England to imagine the colourful procession and noisy fanfare of the event. The richly attired princes, though mere children, are duly noted to be models of aristocratic bearing, befitting their noble birth. The importance of the princes' royal status, evidenced by their regal conduct and appearance, recurs as a common theme in narratives of the hostage taking: their appearance and manner bespeak their nobility, indicating the essentiality of their birthright. Commentators consistently note how the British army treated the boys with great respect, a point calculated to reassure the royalist public in the wake of the French Revolution. Finally, while the head vakeel, Ghulam Ali Khan, may not have uttered the exact words quoted by Dirom, readers of the account and viewers of the images would have perceived Cornwallis' role as the boys' new father.

Robert Home's painting of *Lord Cornwallis Receiving Tipu Saib's Sons as Hostages, Seringapatam, 25 February, 1792* (Fig. 1-1) has become the best-known image of the subject. The large canvas, begun in India and exhibited in the artist's room at the Madras fort before being sent to England, was displayed at the Royal Academy in 1797.[5] Home, the son of an army surgeon, was one of the few artists actually present to depict the Mysorean subjects, and in fact has included himself to the left of the scene, his portfolio under his arm. Prior to becoming official war artist to Cornwallis in 1790, he had trained under Angelica Kauffmann. Certainly the image of the small princes, in Home's work and others, resonates with Kauffmann's famous depiction of Cornelia's children in *Cornelia, Mother of the Gracchi* (c. 1785), where the Roman matron presents her children as her "treasures."

---

[4] Alexander Dirom, *A Narrative of the Campaign in India, which Terminated the War with Tippoo Sultaun, in 1792* (1793; facsimile reprint, New Delhi: Asian Educational Services, 1985), 228-29.

[5] Peter Harrington, *British Artists and War: The Face of Battle in Paintings and Prints, 1700-1914* (London: Greenhill Books; Mechanicsburg, PA: Stackpole Books in association with Brown University Library, 1993), 58. Subscriptions for a print based on the painting were advertised in the Madras press in 1794.

Tipu Sultan's Sons and Images of Paternalism in Late Eighteenth-Century British Art

Fig. 1-1. Robert Home, *Lord Cornwallis Receiving Tipu Saib's Sons as Hostages, Seringapatam, 25 February 1792*, oil on canvas, c. 1792-95. Courtesy of the Council of the National Army Museum, London.

Home's canvas, the most elaborate and apparently the most faithful visual account of the ceremony, is a panoramic scene replete with British and Indian troops in colorful uniforms, as well as elephants, tents, and a view of Seringapatam in the distance. Through the open space in the foreground and his arrangement of the figures, most of whom face the central action, the artist draws our attention to Cornwallis as he reaches with both hands to the youngest prince, Muiz-ud-Din. In turn, the little boy (age eight at the time) gently takes the general's right hand with his own as he steps gracefully toward him. In fact, the prince seems to rush eagerly to Cornwallis; his long, loose, pink and white garment swirls behind him and emphasizes his effeminate, dance-like movements. Several Indian attendants on the right gesture actively, while the British on the left stand solemnly, demonstrating control over their emotions as they observe the event and thereby indicating their civilized and gentlemanly demeanor. Seated on a raised platform behind Muiz-ud-Din, Ghulam Ali Khan stands in for the boys' actual father as he hands them over to their new, surrogate father. The vakeel's gesture indicates his sadness, and therefore Tipu's sadness, at giving up the children: while his right hand reaches toward them, his left hand rests over his heart. The British officials nearest Ghulam Ali Khan convey sympathy for him: one draws his hands together and the other touches his comrade's shoulder, as they both gaze at the sorrowful vakeel. Another Indian attendant, his back to us in the right foreground, covers his face with his hands as if so overcome with emotion that he cannot bear to be seen. Between these expressive figures, Muiz-ud-Din, in his fluttering robe, appears like a delicate wild animal—a bird or a butterfly—that Ghulam Ali Khan has released. While Home draws our attention to the central drama of the boys happily and elegantly entering their term of hostage (particularly to Muiz-ud-Din's expression as he looks affectionately at Cornwallis with sparkling eyes), the overall scene conveys a sense of tension. The British and Indian forces appear to be at a standoff centered around the handover of the boys, and each side holds weapons at the ready. One Indian figure, on camelback at the right, waves his stick in the air—an exuberant gesture which could indicate excitement, encouragement, or anger. Indeed, the British officer standing in the left foreground looks at this man with an expression of concern, as does the artist himself.

The year in which Home's canvas debuted at the Royal Academy saw significant turmoil for the British military. 1797 marked the Spithead and Nore mutinies on Royal Navy ships in April and May, and England appeared to be losing to France in the ongoing war. Images like Home's, and those of other artists discussed below, offered a reassuring view of the military as a good family, rather than an oppressive force against which to rebel. These are images of inclusion and benevolent paternalism, promoting a positive view of the monarchy (represented here by its officers). They demonstrate that one should look to one's father/government for protection. Of course, this implied a *British* father or government, as contemporary viewers would have perceived the boys' real father as a tyrannical ruler, characterized at times as a Muslim fanatic or a bloodthirsty killer. Tipu and his father had taken many British prisoners during the Second Mysore War in the early 1780s. Following the Peace of Mangalore in 1784, all British prisoners were to be released, though according to historian P. J. Marshall, "those that were released quickly spread stories about their barbaric treatment while captives and about the numerous British subjects who remained behind."[6] Several accounts revealed that Tipu had not, in fact, released all his prisoners as he

---

[6] P. J. Marshall, "'Cornwallis Triumphant': War in India and the British Public in the Late Eighteenth Century," in *War, Strategy and International Politics: Essays in Honour of Sir Michael Howard*, ed. Lawrence Freedman et al. (Oxford: Clarendon, 1992), 70.

had agreed to do. Some former captives reported that "younger soldiers and sailors" and all "craftsmen had been [kept] … and forced into Tipu's service. Many of them had been circumcised and had subsequently been seen in Muslim dress." One former midshipman, William Drake, published an account in the *London Gazette* in 1792 wherein he "related how 'several of the European boys were taught dancing in the country style, and forced to dance in female dress before Tippoo.'"[7]

Fig. 1-2. Joseph Grozer after Henry Singleton, *Departure of the Hostages from Seringapatam (Tippoo Sultaun delivering to Gullum Alli the Vakeel his two Sons, who are taking leave of their Brother previously to their departure from Seringapatam)*, engraving, 1793. Courtesy of the Council of the National Army Museum, London.

---

[7] Marshall 70.

Interestingly, Tipu himself was frequently described as effeminate: one account claims that "his bust was corpulent,"[8] and another contemporary description notes that "he was of low stature, corpulent, with high shoulders, and a short thick neck, but his feet and hands were remarkably small" and that he had "small arched eyebrows."[9] This feminized Tipu appears in several visual images of the hostage princes as well. In Henry Singleton's *Departure of the Hostages from Seringapatam* (Fig. 1-2), the two young princes, dressed in white robes, say their last goodbyes to their father as they turn to leave the palace. It is highly unlikely that any Western observer witnessed the scene when the boys left their father,[10] but artists took the opportunity nonetheless to depict Tipu and his attendants as emotional, effeminate males in contrast to the princes, who appear calm and resigned to their fate. In Singleton's image, Tipu and his officials wear garments resembling the high-waisted gowns then fashionable among European women, along with several heavy strands of beads. One guard, at the right, sports a uniform recalling the "skeleton suit," an outfit just becoming popular for young boys in England. Though some Indian men's clothing of the 1790s may have resembled European dresses or juvenile wear to a small degree, Singleton's image would have reinforced the perception of such men as feminine or childlike. Both of these associations also serve to indicate Tipu's unfitness as a father for his sons, who, in all of the images where they are shown with Cornwallis, appear pleased to become wards of the British. Mather Brown's painting of *Lord Cornwallis Receiving the Sons of Tipu Sultan as Hostages* (Fig. 1-3), for instance, replaces the figure of Tipu with that of Ghulam Ali Khan on the left, and shows the boys happily stepping away with Cornwallis, hand in hand, from their entourage of elephants and lavishly dressed attendants.[11] They

---

[8] Quoted in Colley 298.

[9] "Major Allan's Account of his Interview with the Princes in the Palace of Seringapatam, and of finding the Body of the late Tippoo Sultaun," in Alexander Beatson, *A View of the Origin and Conduct of the War with Tippoo Sultaun* (London: 1800), Appendix XLII: cxxxi.

[10] Joachim K. Bautze, *Interaction of Cultures: Indian and Western Painting 1780-1910* (Alexandria: Art Services International, 1998), 147.

[11] Constance McPhee argues that, in various images, Brown has connected Tipu to Richard III (sometimes through the figure of his lame vakeel) and therefore has presented him as the villain in an eighteenth-century version of the Little Princes in the Tower story. McPhee claims that Brown's images "suggest that the sultan was a scheming, ignoble father and thoughtless husband who happily turned his young sons over to his enemies just as Richard had callously consigned his own nephews to the Tower" (211). Her argument is persuasive, but considers only one artist out of several who depicted these events. The story of the princes in the Tower is a

are clearly being led toward civilization (indicated by the rows of British officers standing at the right) and away from their previous "barbaric" lifestyle.

Fig. 1-3. Daniel Orme after Mather Brown, *Lord Cornwallis Receiving the Sons of Tipu Sultan as Hostages*, engraving, c.1793. Anne S. K. Brown Military Collection, Brown University Library.

In contrast to Home's and Brown's detailed, descriptive scenes, an anonymous print of the same subject, published by Robert Sayer in 1792, eliminates the regalia and elephants to focus on the main characters involved (Fig. 1-4). Here, the British army is represented by only three soldiers standing behind Cornwallis. One, a very flat-looking figure carrying a bayonet, appears more like a toy soldier than a human being, and the artist may in fact have based these figures on toy models.

---

clear precedent for the Mysorean narrative, though not one which is evident in all of the representations. Even in Brown's images, it is not clear that Tipu "happily" turned over his sons to the British. See Constance C. McPhee, "Tipu Sultan of Mysore and British Medievalism in the Paintings of Mather Brown," in *Orientalism Transposed: The Impact of the Colonies on British Culture*, ed. Julie F. Codell and Dianne Sachko Macleod (Aldershot: Ashgate, 1998), 202-19.

Cornwallis himself is young and slim, an inaccurate representation. Tipu's vakeel hands the boys to the general in a gesture of submission, watched by another, androgynous, Indian figure standing behind them. This unusual figure may represent one of the boys' mothers, neither of whom

Fig. 1-4. Anonymous, *Tippoo Saib's Two Sons deliver'd up to Lord Cornwallis*, hand-coloured print, 1792. Anne S. K. Brown Military Collection, Brown University Library.

Tipu Sultan's Sons and Images of Paternalism in Late Eighteenth-Century British Art

was present at the ceremony. In fact, Muiz-ud-Din's mother reputedly "died of fright and apprehension" after the British attack on Seringapatam, a story which enhanced contemporary interest in the youngest prince.[12] In this rather crude image (compared to representations by Home, Brown, and Singleton), the boys step from "nature," indicated by a palm tree, toward "culture," symbolized by the army and its tents. The empty tent in the center, though likely meant to be part of the British military encampment, reinforces the idea that the boys have left their home, and are now dependent on Cornwallis as their new parent.

Images like this print, as well the paintings by Home and Brown, also offer an interesting inversion of allegorical representations of Britannia and the East, such as Spiridone Roma's 1778 ceiling painting *The East Offering Its Riches to Britannia* from East India House. Roma's composition employs the traditional formula of female figures representing continents or nations. Here, the East, or India, holds up strings of pearls to Britannia. In contrast, the military images replace such female figures with contemporary male individuals. Cornwallis now stands in for Britannia, and the two princes embody the "riches of the East," duly offered up by Tipu or his vakeel representing "India."

Muiz-ud-Din (Fig. 1-5), supposedly the sultan's favorite son and his intended heir, was described by Major Dirom as "remarkably fair, with regular features, a small round face, large full eyes, and a more animated countenance" than his older brother, who was said to be "rather dark in his colour, with thick lips, a small flattish nose, and a long thoughtful countenance."[13] While such differences between the two boys are not evident in visual accounts, artists often depicted them both with lighter skin than either their attendants or other members of their family. In the anonymous print, Cornwallis and the British soldiers are pale white (in fact, in the print illustrated here, their skin has been coloured with white pigment) and the Indians are dark, although where Muiz-ud-Din's hand touches that of Cornwallis, his skin takes on the same hue as the general's, as if he is becoming white upon contact with a European. The print seems to indicate visually that the boys, once under the paternal care of the British, will become European in their taste and conduct, a notion shown by their literally becoming whiter once they have a "new" European father.[14] In fact, during their stay at Madras while hostages, the princes

---

[12] Dirom 230.
[13] Dirom 229-30.
[14] This notion counters the contemporary idea that British "nabobs" turned black after living in India. See, for instance, the 1797 print of "Count Rupee in Hyde

were "anglicized" by being taken to performances of Handel's *Judas Maccabeus, Messiah,* and *Esther*, as well as amateur dramatic productions. They were also treated to European-style dancing in the form of a minuet, a cotillion, and a Scottish strathspey at a party given by Lady Oakley, the wife of the Governor of Madras. In return, the princes hosted a dinner "à la Seringapatam" for Governor and Lady Oakley.[15] Again, their treatment at the hands of their captors inverts their father's treatment of his British prisoners, who were made to perform Indian dances, apparently against their will.

Fig. 1-5. John Smart, *Muiz-ud-Deen*, graphite, 1794. © Copyright the Trustees of the British Museum.

Park" (illustrated in E. M. Collingham, *Imperial Bodies: The Physical Experience of the Raj, c.1800-1947* [Cambridge: Polity, 2001], 35).
[15] W. S. Seton-Karr, *Madras Courier*, 16 August 1792; quoted in Anne Buddle, *The Tiger and the Thistle: Tipu Sultan and the Scots in India 1760-1800* (Edinburgh: National Gallery of Scotland, 1999), 33.

Tipu Sultan's Sons and Images of Paternalism in Late
Eighteenth-Century British Art

The hostage images rely on precedents such as Francis Hayman's *Surrender of Montreal to General Amherst*, painted for Vauxhall Gardens in 1760-61. Here, Amherst receives the vanquished citizens of Montreal, including several children, with a gesture of welcome and acceptance. Hayman's popular image inspired contemporary viewers to sympathetic response in the face of such magnanimity,[16] as did the images of Cornwallis with the young princes. Both Hayman's painting and the Mysorean subjects also recall an episode from the classical past, that of Alexander the Great with the family of Darius, an event represented by Charles Le Brun in 1660-61 and engraved later in the seventeenth century.[17] When Alexander defeated Darius at the Battle of Issus, Darius fled, leaving his family behind. Though Alexander could have killed them, he demonstrated clemency toward the family of his enemy. The late eighteenth-century public would have appreciated references to the great conqueror Alexander, especially as the Greek hero had designs on India as well. While Alexander never controlled the subcontinent, the British believed they could improve upon his success in that part of the world.

In 1799, General Baird also demonstrated Alexander-like qualities toward Tipu's family after storming the palace at Seringapatam to end the Fourth and final Mysore War. During the siege, Muiz-ud-Din and another son surrendered themselves, unaware that their father had already been killed.[18] This brief war had been sparked when the British intercepted a letter to Tipu from no less an adversary than Napoleon Bonaparte. The letter, reproduced in Alexander Beatson's contemporary narrative of the Mysore Wars, proclaims that Napoleon and his army (then in Cairo) were "full of the desire of delivering you from the iron yoke of England."[19] In fact, Tipu had a long history of aligning himself with the French, be their government a monarchy or a republic. In 1787, he sent ambassadors to Louis XVI to appeal, unsuccessfully, for assistance against the British. After the fall of the monarchy, Tipu, who had a handful of French troops at Seringapatam, experimented with contemporary French political ideals in an allegiance with the Republic. The French soldiers at Mysore formed a Jacobin club in 1798, where they gathered to "swear hatred to all Kings

---

[16] David H. Solkin, *Painting for Money: The Visual Arts and the Public Sphere in Eighteenth-Century England* (New Haven and London: Yale UP, 1992), 199. Hayman's modello for this lost painting is illustrated in Solkin 192.
[17] See Solkin 196-97 on Hayman's work in comparison to that of Le Brun.
[18] The other hostage prince from 1792, Abdul Khalik, was elsewhere defending the palace during the siege.
[19] See Beatson, Appendix VII: xxxi.

except Tippoo Sultaun," whom they even called "Citizen Tippoo."[20] Tipu's pattern of seeking French support, even while his identity changed from royalist to "Citizen," certainly would have alarmed the British and supported the stereotype of Eastern rulers as shifty and deceitful.[21] Once again, Tipu can be seen as a poor father, to his subjects and to his sons.

The figure of Warren Hastings offered another paternal image against which Cornwallis, and later Baird, would have positioned themselves. Governor-General of India from 1774-87, Hastings stood trial during the Third Mysore War, his conduct causing him to be reviled as a bad "father," this time of the East India Company itself. Cornwallis' benevolence to his rival's family, akin to that of Alexander, revealed to the British public that the Company could, in fact, act as good fathers in the subcontinent without abusing their powers. Significantly, the East India Company particularly needed to justify its actions at this moment, as it was undergoing a renewal of its charter during the Mysore Wars. In the 1780s, the Company itself had been accused of atrocities, particularly against women; one officer, Henry Oakes, wrote that Tipu's treatment of his British captives "was evidently founded upon principles of retaliation...the unjustifiable behaviour of the Company's army goes a considerable way in justification of that of the enemy."[22] While the Company later ordered that Oakes retract his statement, which he did, popular opinion still held that the British were, at times, less than civil toward Indians.

Cornwallis and Baird needed to be presented as competent leaders, in control of their own soldiers, if they were to control Mysore. When his army stormed the palace in 1799, Baird expressed concern for the safety of Tipu's family, since he knew his men would be difficult to control. At this point, the army had heard that Tipu was killing European prisoners, and the soldiers were ready to seek revenge by slaughtering occupants of the palace. Baird, himself a former prisoner at Seringapatam, proved to be like his predecessor Cornwallis when he insisted that Tipu's sons be brought out of the palace to surrender, so that their family would be safe. Of

---

[20] Col. M. Wood and J. Salmond, *A Review of the Origin, Progress and Result of the late decisive War in Mysore* (London, 1800), 41-56; quoted in Buddle 33.
[21] While claiming to be a supporter of the republic, Tipu did not relinquish power over his subjects. Also, he retained emblems of European kingship in his palace, probably unbeknownst to his Jacobin residents. A pair of plaques bearing the portraits of Louis XVI and Marie Antoinette, given to Tipu's father, was found in his palace in 1799.
[22] Henry Oakes, *An Authentic Narrative of the English who were taken Prisoners on the Reduction of Bednor by Tippoo Saib* (London, 1785), quoted in Colley 295.

course, Baird also demanded they tell him Tipu's whereabouts, but the boys apparently did not know where their father was, nor that he had already been killed.

Fig. 1-6. Anthony Cardon after Henry Singleton, *The Surrender of Two Sons of Tippoo Sultan*, engraving, 1802. Anne S. K. Brown Military Collection, Brown University Library.

In Henry Singleton's representation of *The Surrender of Two Sons of Tippoo Sultaun* (Fig. 1-6), the boys descend the palace steps while their father's troops watch from the right. Two soldiers in the Indian regiment are European, presumably French, and Singleton has included a group of sepoys among the British ranks on the left. The unusual figure seated on the ground at the lower left is reminiscent of the Native American in Benjamin West's *Death of General Wolfe* (1770); perhaps he functions here as a thoughtful observer who contemplates the passing of an old regime into new hands, symbolized here by the boys passing literally into the hands of General Baird. Major Alexander Allan, seen here leading the boys toward Baird, recalled in his account of the surrender that he entered the palace with a white flag of truce, and was received by the princes "as soon as a carpet could be spread for the purpose."[23] Even under siege, the

---

[23] Allan in Beatson, Appendix XLII: cxxix.

princes are noted to retain their good manners and proper sense of decorum. Allan, upon recognizing Muiz-ud-Din, whom he knew following the Third Mysore War, relates that he was moved to "the strongest emotions of compassion." Once Allan was able to convince the princes that their surrender would save their family, the boys were led out of the palace where they were received by Baird and conducted to the army's headquarters under "the compliment of presented arms."[24]

Compositionally, Singleton's *Surrender* is remarkably like his earlier French Revolutionary image, *The Destruction of the Bastille* (Fig. 1-7). In the Indian scene, Singleton has replaced the Bastille with the fortified wall of Tipu's palace, and the gateway from which the French prisoners emerge has become the large doorway through which the sultan's sons have walked. Singleton thus offers us an interpretation of Tipu's palace as a place of imprisonment, and his sons as innocent victims whom the assembled troops have liberated. As David Bindman points out, Singleton's Bastille print "is the only British work to have come to light which offers an heroic view of the attack on the Bastille from the years 1789-92, when such a subject would have been acceptable."[25] The same heroic spirit infuses the Seringapatam scene, although in this case, the fighting has ceased: the princes come out peacefully while the attackers watch. "Citizen Tippoo" had by this point become a friend of Napoleon, usurper of power, and in the eyes of the British remained an Oriental despot whose lavish palace could seem no better than a prison for its occupants.

While Singleton's image is the best known and most reproduced representation of the 1799 surrender, a work by Thomas Stothard makes an interesting comparison, as it is one of the few images where Tipu's sons are shown with women. *The Surrender of the Children of Tippoo Sultaun on the Fourth of May 1799*, also known as *The Departure of the Sons of Tipu Sultaun from the Zenana*, was published as a colored engraving by James Daniell in 1800 (Fig. 1-8). This very inaccurate scene depicts the boys, much too young, "leaving the zenana [women's quarters]

---

[24] Allan in Beatson, Appendix XLII: cxxx.
[25] David Bindman, *The Shadow of the Guillotine: Britain and the French Revolution* (London: The British Museum, 1989), 91. Bindman also notes that the composition of the Bastille image is based upon a famous French medal commemorating the event, presumably the kind that circulated among Revolutionary supporters in England. I thank K. Dian Kriz for bringing this print to my attention.

with numerous ladies in flowing empire gowns weeping around them."[26] As Mildred Archer observes, Stothard "seems to be confusing the surrender of the hostages in 1792 with the surrender to Baird in 1799."[27]

Fig. 1-7. William Nutter after Henry Singleton, *The Destruction of the Bastille*, engraving, 1792. © Copyright the Trustees of the British Museum.

The image is notable, though, in its sentimental attempt to indicate the sadness involved as the children are taken away from their family, while still presenting the British soldiers as the boys' rightful guardians. The princes, while not overjoyed at having to leave their female relatives, do not display the same emotional response to the situation, and in fact remain quite stoic. The Indian boys and women appear European in complexion and facial features, whereas their male attendants, particularly the two men standing in the shadows on the left, are once again much darker, their bulging eyes and thick lips likening them to caricatures of Africans from this period. The older boy, on the right, holds the hand of an officer who has already begun to step toward the doorway. While the prince looks with some concern to the grieving women, he doesn't reach

---

[26] Mildred Archer, *India and British Portraiture 1770-1825* (London and New York: Sotheby Parke Bernet, 1979), 427.
[27] Archer 427.

back to them, indicating that, like the British men, he has mastered his emotions. The younger boy also demonstrates self-control: though his sister (?) clutches his wrist, he does not reciprocate. His hand, silhouetted against a shadow, hangs limply.

Fig. 1-8. James Daniell after Thomas Stothard, *The Surrender of the Children of Tippoo Sultaun on the Fourth of May 1799 (The Departure of the Sons of Tipu Sultaun from the Zenana)*, engraving, 1800. Anne S. K. Brown Military Collection, Brown University Library.

In this unusual image, I believe viewers are meant to sympathize with the women, whose family is being torn apart. But we are also meant to understand that the British officers are kind and gentle, and will provide a better home for these male children than the feminine environment of the palace. Beatson's narrative describes how Abdul Khalik (who surrendered the next morning) "betrayed not the smallest symptom of emotion" when told that his father was probably dead. Once the prince heard that Tipu was, in fact, among the victims of the siege, he received the news "with perfect indifference."[28] Such accounts attest to the boys' readiness to assume their place alongside the British soldiers once again, and Singleton's and Stothard's images declare that they have accepted, even welcomed, their fate.

---

[28] Beatson 147.

These images, as well as those of the earlier surrender scene, should be considered in another context of broken families—African slave families torn apart by European colonial powers. The years of the Third and Fourth Mysore Wars also witnessed the height of the abolitionist movement in Britain; George Morland's *The Slave Trade* of 1788 (engraved in 1791; Fig. 1-9) stands as a powerful reminder of the violence wrought on African families. First exhibited at the Royal Academy in London under the title *Execrable Human Traffick*, Morland's painting was inspired by William Collins' *The Slave Trade: A Poem Written in the Year 1788*.[29] Collins wrote of an African chief whose family was ruptured by British slave traders; Morland's image shows one white trader brandishing a stick over the chief's head as the African man pleads, hands clasped, for his wife and son. A second trader leads away the chief's wife, whose small son clings to her with an anguished expression. The message here is clear: the cruel and cold-hearted British brutally tear apart a loving family. While drawing upon current conceptions of the "noble savage," Morland's image and Collins' verses speak specifically to the importance of the family and the idea of a devoted father.

Fig. 1-9. John Raphael Smith after George Morland, *The Slave Trade*, engraving, 1791. Davison Art Center, Wesleyan University. Photo: R. J. Phil.

---

[29] William Collins, *The Slave Trade: A Poem Written in the Year 1788* (London, 1793); see Hugh Honour, *The Image of the Black in Western Art* vol. 4, part 1 (Cambridge, MA and London: Harvard UP, 1989), 66-71.

Enslaved African families rarely appeared in paintings from this period (Morland's work forms a notable exception), though the separation of African parents and children remained, as James G. Basker notes, "a cruel fact and a literary commonplace" in late eighteenth-century abolitionist verse.[30] Mary Stockdale's "Fidelle; or, the Negro Child," published in 1798, comprises one of many works from this period that focus on the painful theme. Stockdale's Fidelle speaks particularly of her own father's anguish after losing his daughter:

> My father now, unhappy man!
>   Weeps for his lov'd Fidelle,
> And wonders much that Christians can
>   Poor negroes buy and sell:
> O had you heard him beg and pray,
>   And seen his looks so wild!
> He cried, "O let me bless this day;
>   O spare my darling child!"[31]

While much abolitionist literature makes a sentimental appeal to the reader on behalf of the black family, and, like Morland's painting, foregrounds the sundering of African familial bonds by corrupt and cruel Europeans, the Mysorean images succeed in presenting the Indian princes' *real* family as the corrupt family, and the British as their (literally) upstanding and benevolent surrogate father(s). The princes always appear happier with the British than with their own Indian relatives; such visual propaganda mitigated concern over a native family forcibly broken apart.

After defeating Tipu and removing his family from Seringapatam, the British restored the Rajah of Mysore to the throne, though the Company retained actual control over the region. The princes were taken with their relatives to live in the British fortress at Vellore, where English observers duly noted their quarters as more magnificent than their previous accommodations in their father's palace. British accounts of the end of the Mysore Wars point out that Tipu's family received "a more munificent maintenance" than what they had "enjoyed during the late reign."[32] Of course, it was the East India Company that now enjoyed munificence in the region once the Tiger of Mysore was dead and the British dominated his land. The princes, seemingly docile under British control, would later

---

[30] James G. Basker, ed., *Amazing Grace: An Anthology of Poems about Slavery, 1660-1810* (New Haven and London: Yale UP, 2002), 536.
[31] Mary Stockdale, "Fidelle; or, the Negro Child" from *The Effusions of the Heart: Poems* (London, 1798), in Basker 536-37.
[32] Beatson 220-21.

assist in provoking the Vellore Mutiny of 1806, where sepoys stationed at the fortress killed nearly one hundred British troops. Before this, however, sentimental images of the little boys helped elevate Cornwallis and Baird to heroic stature as benevolent fathers and glorious leaders. Just as the boys had been treated as currency between the British and their greatest foe in India, pictures of them became a kind of currency too, of ideological work carried out far from their own home. A poem entitled "Cornwallis Triumphant," published in December 1792, ends with a verse considering the fate of the princes:

> Drink a health to brave Cornwallis, and all his valiant men,
>   And to all bold commanders who strive their country's rights to gain,
> And Tippoo's two sons, as Hostages we have got.
>   Should they arrive in England, who knows what may be their lot.[33]

In retrospect, we know what the "lot" of the princes entailed, for they did arrive in England, in painting after painting, and print after print, successfully denigrating their father's image in the eyes of the British public and demonstrating that the East India Company constituted a better parent to India than its own native rulers.

Works Cited

Archer, Mildred. *India and British Portraiture 1770-1825*. London and New York: Sotheby Parke Bernet, 1979.

Basker, James G., ed. *Amazing Grace: An Anthology of Poems about Slavery, 1660-1810*. New Haven and London: Yale UP, 2002.

Bautze, Joachim K. *Interaction of Cultures: Indian and Western Painting 1780-1910*. Alexandria: Art Services International, 1998.

Beatson, Alexander. *A View of the Origin and Conduct of the War with Tippoo Sultaun*. London: 1800.

Bindman, David. *The Shadow of the Guillotine: Britain and the French Revolution*. London: The British Museum, 1989.

Buddle, Anne. *The Tiger and the Thistle: Tipu Sultan and the Scots in India 1760-1800*. Edinburgh: National Gallery of Scotland, 1999.

Colley, Linda. *Captives: The Story of Britain's Pursuit of Empire and How Its Soldiers and Civilians were Held Captive by the Dream of Global Supremacy, 1600-1850*. New York: Pantheon, 2002.

---

[33] Quoted in Marshall 62.

Collingham, E. M. *Imperial Bodies: The Physical Experience of the Raj, c.1800-1947*. Cambridge: Polity, 2001.
Collins, William. *The Slave Trade: A Poem Written in the Year 1788*. London: 1793.
Dirom, Alexander. *A Narrative of the Campaign in India, which Terminated the War with Tippoo Sultaun, in 1792*. 1793. Facsimile reprint, New Delhi: Asian Educational Services, 1985.
Harrington, Peter. *British Artists and War: The Face of Battle in Paintings and Prints, 1700-1914*. London: Greenhill Books; Mechanicsburg, PA: Stackpole Books in association with Brown University Library, 1993.
Honour, Hugh. *The Image of the Black in Western Art*. Vol. 4, part 1. Cambridge, MA and London: Harvard UP, 1989.
Marshall, P. J. "'Cornwallis Triumphant': War in India and the British Public in the Late Eighteenth Century." In *War, Strategy, and International Politics: Essays in Honour of Sir Michael Howard*, ed. Lawrence Freedman et al., 57-74. Oxford: Clarendon, 1992.
McPhee, Constance C. "Tipu Sultan of Mysore and British Medievalism in the Paintings of Mather Brown." In *Orientalism Transposed: The Impact of the Colonies on British Culture*, ed. Julie F. Codell and Dianne Sachko Macleod, 202-19. Aldershot: Ashgate, 1998.
Solkin, David. *Painting for Money: The Visual Arts and the Public Sphere in Eighteenth-Century England*. New Haven and London: Yale UP, 1992.
Teltscher, Kate. *India Inscribed: European and British Writing on India, 1600-1800*. Delhi: Oxford UP, 1995.

Chapter Two

Richard Edgeworth as Parent and Educator

Brian Hollingworth, University of Derby

Richard Lovell Edgeworth (1744-1817) was married four times and begat 22 children. His marriages in themselves were often of a spectacular nature. His first wife was Anna Maria Elers, one of three pretty daughters in the house where he was lodging while studying at Oxford. The couple ran away together and were married at Gretna Green. Their first child was born before Richard was twenty.

From Richard's point of view this marriage was unhappy and he soon fell in love with another woman, Honora Sneyd. He went briefly to France to avoid all temptation to be unfaithful, and was probably relieved rather than heartbroken when Anna died after childbirth to their third child. At any rate he married Honora only four months after Anna's death.

When Honora was herself dying of T.B., realising that her husband could not live without a wife, she advised him to marry her sister Elizabeth. Honora died in 1790, and Richard duly complied with her dying wishes, despite the fact that he was marrying his deceased wife's sister, barely on the edge of legality.

Elizabeth herself died of T.B. in 1797, and within a year he was married to Frances Beaufort, who, at 29 to his 53, was a year younger than Edgeworth's eldest surviving child, Maria, the famous novelist. His fourth wife survived him by many years.

By Anna, Edgeworth had 5 children, by Honora 2, by Elizabeth 9, by Frances 6. There were 12 girls and 10 boys. 2 died as babies. Typically of the times another 6 died before they were 30. His last child died in 1897, 133 years after his first child was born.

The remarkable thing is that Edgeworth put as much energy into childrearing as he did into procreation, developed his own methods of education, and, after he returned to Ireland in 1782, educated all the children from his three marriages at home. Moreover, he encouraged his daughter Maria in her many educational publications. It is, as you may know, debatable how far their most famous production *Practical Education* published in 1800 is authored by Richard or Maria, but certainly he was a major contributor. In 1808 he published the book which is definitely his own, *Professional Education*. Edgeworth was also in the early 1800s a Commissioner on the board set up to "inquire into the education of the People of Ireland". This in addition to being heavily involved in bog reclamation in Ireland and pursuing his private hobby of developing a telegraph system. He was also concerned with designing carriages, and his local church steeple. The man seemed indefatigable.

How successful he was as an educator, behind all this activity, is no doubt open to question. We may wonder how far his children appreciated his efforts. There is some evidence that not all of them were as enthusiastic as his famous daughter Maria, who completed his *Memoirs*, and eulogistically emphasised therein his virtues as a landlord and as a teacher. And another question, particularly relevant to the subject of this conference, would be how far his educational ideals were actually influenced in a positive way by the theories of "romantic" thinkers whose influence in Britain coincided with the time of his maturity and the bringing up of his children.

Such questions are underlined when we consider the fate of his eldest son, Richard, who was born in 1764. This is the one child whom Edgeworth publicly proclaimed to have failed in educating and significantly he blamed the influence of the great Romantic educator Rousseau for this failure. The boy proved headstrong and, according to Edgeworth's *Memoirs* "self-willed from a spirit of independence which had been inculcated by his early education, and which he cherished the more from the inexperience of his own powers."[1]

Edgeworth had taken his son to France, during his heroically self-imposed separation from Honora Sneyd, and, while in Paris, he had introduced the boy in person to Rousseau. But he blamed himself for basing Richard's education upon "the mistaken principles of Rousseau"[2] and grew so exasperated with the boy that he sent him to a Catholic Seminary where, nevertheless, Richard proved "more than a match for his Catholic instructors", by arguing about the view of creation which was presented to him by his teachers.

---

[1] Memoirs, 1844, 174-175.
[2] Ibid, 174.

His son's subsequent history, at least as told by the Edgeworth family and British commentators, (is there a more favourable American version, I wonder?) confirms the failure of his upbringing. In 1779, he went to sea [3], the favourite occupation of family misfits. In 1783 he deserted from the Navy [4] and Edgeworth refused to let him come home. Richard then went off to South Carolina where he compounded his faults by marrying an American Methodist, Elizabeth Knight. When he visited his relatives in 1795 he was given money to set up as a farmer, but died shortly after his return to America. Edgeworth's comments on hearing of the death of his first born were hardly laced with paternal feeling:

"All that he received from me in two years, £2000, was spent and his way of life had become such as promised no happiness to himself or his family – it is therefore better for both that he has retired from the scene." [5]

So, when established in Ireland and educating the rest of his numerous brood, we can scarcely expect to find in his methods that romantic emphasis on the development of the individual in freedom which marks Rousseau and much romantic educational theory of the late eighteenth and the nineteenth century – no wandering in the woods, sitting by Walden pond, or getting close to nature for Edgeworth's children. Edgeworth's aim, among the black bogs of Central Ireland, was always to tame nature, rather than to commune with it. Similarly, another crucial exploration of romantic education – "the authenticity of individual emotion" and the importance of nurturing the child's imagination – is entirely absent from Edgeworth's educational lexicon. As late as 1816 he and Maria published together a book, "Readings on Poetry", for children. The excerpts he chooses are entirely pre-romantic in substance and in tone, and the comments upon them are antagonistic to the Romantic poets and show no concept of the significance of the imagination. We must remember that one of his best friends, close to him in temperament and ideology, was Erasmus Darwin, bestselling poet of the 1790's, author of *The Botanic Garden* (a precursor of his grandson's theories of evolution) – a poet whose ornate whimsicality had been by 1816 eclipsed and ridiculed by the Lake Poets and their converts.

Nevertheless I think we can see in Edgeworth's approach to educating his children at least two factors which, with the benefit of hindsight, might broadly be called "romantic". Firstly he held an optimistic belief in the

---

[3] Butler, 51.
[4] Ibid., 99.
[5] Ibid., 106-107.

innate ability and enthusiasm of children, male or female, to learn if encouraged to do so by sympathetic environment and teachers. Edgeworth was ever the optimist, had no belief in original sin, and expected his children to be curious about themselves and the world. Secondly he had an unshakeable belief in the democracy of knowledge, and, within that belief, a conviction that practical skills were at least as valuable as the traditional academic and "classical" education. These views he actually developed, not from any romantic theorist, but rather from personal experience. His close association with the Lunar Society, that group of men, centred on Birmingham, which included the manufacturers Matthew Boulton and Josiah Wedgewood, Erasmus Darwin and later James Watt and Joseph Priestley, had convinced him that the traditional barriers of an aristocratic and classical education were an obstacle to true learning and advancement. The members of the Lunar Society were practical men, often "self-educated" with independent, latitudinarian attitudes to religion, and radical convictions in politics. These men prided themselves on their "practicality" and their eager search for knowledge owed nothing to romanticism. Nevertheless their instinctive assumption that education and learning were personally beneficial for all, whatever their social rank or position, and that, given the opportunity, all would respond positively to them, fit easily with certain aspects of Romantic ideology.

For the purposes of this paper, I will not elaborate on Edgeworth's optimistic child-centred approach to learning. It is set out attractively in *Practical Education*, a text still worth reading. The book's liberal approach still has much to say, at least to contemporary educators in England whose current passion for testing everything that moves, seems to have more in common with Thomas Gradgrind than Jacques Rousseau. But I'd like to say a bit more about the consequences of his belief in the democracy of knowledge, and how it affected the education of his own children. It is interesting to me, especially, because it is fictionally illustrated in one of Maria Edgeworth's novels, and also because it links Edgeworth directly to my home town of Derby.

In Maria Edgeworth's novel *Patronage*, which clearly has strong autobiographical associations, two families are contrasted. One family is called the Percy's (obviously intended to represent the Edgeworths), the other is called the Falconer's. The Percy's turn their back on promotion through patronage, and the father devotes his male children through their education to private virtue and public service. So Alfred becomes a lawyer, the significantly named Erasmus becomes a doctor, and Godfrey becomes an officer in the army. The Falconer's, on the other hand, are ruthless in their ambition and lap up patronage. Cunningham Falconer becomes a politician's unscrupulous secretary, and Buckhurst, despite no genuine Christian beliefs and a dissolute lifestyle, becomes a Church of England clergyman.

It is clear that Edgeworth employed the same arbitrary, but socially dedicated pattern to the career of several of his own sons. Henry was sent to Edinburgh to train as a doctor, though unhappily he seems to have had a breakdown and died at thirty. Sneyd was trained in England and settled down there, as a lawyer. But, most interesting of all, and quite out of keeping with the habits of landed families at the time, or indeed the characterisation in Maria's novel, son William was deliberately trained as an engineer and worked on the new railways and roads which were being surveyed and built at the time.

As an important part of their education, it was customary for Edgeworth to visit with his children, or send his children to stay with, William Strutt in Derby. Strutt was a textile mill owner, and Edgeworth had made friends with him as early as 1785 through Erasmus Darwin.[6] When he visited Darwin in Derby, he also saw Strutt, and after Darwin died in 1802, their close friendship continued.[7] Through this contact he made sure that his children – girls as well as boys quite often – knew something of the new industrialism which was developing in the country, and had the opportunity to visit factories and study the new industrial processes. Edgeworth's children came to have a very positive attitude towards industrialisation and the benefits it could bring.[8] There is nothing of the horror of getting ones hands dirty which so marks the class-ridden classical emphasis of early 19th Century traditional education in Britain. Nor is there any suggestion that practical education is inferior to the academic. Indeed "practical" is always a term of high esteem in the Edgworthian vocabulary. Hence my claim for "the democracy of knowledge" in Edgeworth's educational theories.

William actually began his career as an engineer in Strutt's mill[9] and there is every indication that this thoroughly suited Edgeworth, who was

---

[6] Letter of William Strutt to Maria Edgeworth, 1st March 1819: MS36-1947: Fitzwilliam Museum Cambridge.

[7] Clarke, 134. There is some evidence that it is Edgeworth who, in conversation with Strutt and Erasmus Darwin, 'invented' the fire-proof iron-framed mills of the early 19th century, which in turn led, I understand, to American skyscrapers, Letter from Sneyd Edgeworth to Honora Edgeworth, his half-sister, 2nd January 1811: Beaufort –Edgeworth Letters, National Library of Ireland, Dublin, M.S. 13176.

[8] See letter, Charlotte Edgeworth to Mary Sneyd, 25th September 1802: Butler-Edgeworth Letters No 303: National Library of Ireland, Dublin, M.S. 10166-7.

[9] Clarke, 134.

an inventor in his own right and once described himself as an "inveterate mechanic." Maria herself kept up an affectionate correspondence with Strutt after her father's death which indicates something of how William's career developed. There is hardly a letter which does not mention William, and she describes how he was employed by the mayor and aldermen of Stockton to see whether the Tees was, or could be, navigable – a poignant recapitulation of his father's employment on the Rhone at Lyon during his time in France. He was later involved with the survey of Ireland "making roads and plans for bridges".[10] Strutt, for his part, seems to have been in constant close contact with the young man, and, when William brought back a manuscript which Maria had sent Strutt for comment on its technical accuracy, he remarks that her brother himself is "well qualified to supply any other observations and corrections that you may require."[11]

Sadly, while engaged in roadbuilding in Armagh in 1829, William developed pneumonia and became yet another of Edgeworth's children to die young – in his mid thirties.[12] Yet his career, and the pride which the family took in it, testifies to Richard Edgeworth's radical view of the role, function and purpose of education – a view basically democratic in outlook.

I suppose, after all, it could be argued that here is a further sign that Edgeworth was not a "romantic" at all, since romanticism in Britain is most frequently associated with the rejection of industrialisation and of all its works. There is no "Newton's night" thinking in Edgeworth. On the contrary, he was an enthusiast for mechanical innovations of all kinds and a friend of some of the greatest industrialists of his generation. Nevertheless, wherever we try to place his educational philosophy, he remains an intriguing educational figure, and a very attractive object of study for educational theorists today – idiosyncratic, stubbornly egocentric, but alive to the potentialities of children and to the opportunities of the emerging industrial society.

---

[10] Letter from Maria Edgeworth to William Strutt, 22nd April1823: MS27-1947: Fitzwilliam Museum, Cambridge.
[11] Letter from William Strutt to Maria Edgeworth, 17th November 1823: MS 38-1947: Fitzwilliam Museum Cambridge.
[12] Letter from Maria Edgeworth to William Strutt, 29th May 1829: MS 31-1947: Fitzwilliam Museum Cambridge.

Works Cited

Butler, Marilyn. *Maria Edgeworth*. Oxford, 1972.
Clarke, D. *The Ingenious Mr. Edgeworth*. London, 1965.
Edgeworth Richard. *Memoirs (3rd Edition)*. London, 1844.

Coda

It may be interesting to point out an important context in which Maria Edgeworth's writing echoes that aspect of her father's educational ideas which I have been emphasising here.

Maria wrote two sets of stories which are theoretically linked together.

She published stories called "Tales of Fashionable Life" (two series) which, as the title implies, deal with upper class life – the world of Jane Austen or Fanny Burney, or indeed most respectable literature of the time. She also published "Popular Tales", which deal with the mercantile and manufacturing classes. One of these, for example, implicitly informs the reader that the hero is William Strutt since it is set in Derby, and another is clearly based on details in the early life of her friend Sir Humphry Davy in Cornwall.

Three features stand out about these stories. Firstly, basing her ideas on French models, she was probably the first British author to designate her stories as "tales". She was, of course, shortly to be followed by Scott with his "Tales of My Landlord", "Tales of the Crusaders" etc and the idea has been copied by many others.

Secondly, these stories do not just provide a different subject matter, they are aimed at a different readership. "Popular Tales" are aimed at an audience of the people, as its preface (written, as was customary in her publications, by Richard Edgeworth) makes clear. This "popular" audience is the newly emerging, newly educated, middle classes of the industrial revolution. Edgeworth is one of the first serious novelists to realise that they exist and deliberately to cater for them.

Thirdly, it is noticeable that whilst she depicts "fashionable life" negatively, if conventionally, as full of hypocrisy, idleness and dissipation, the heroes of her "Popular Tales", the Strutts of this world, are a much more admirable group of people. She clearly shares her father's attitudes towards this brave new world of industry and commerce.

The Tales, then, provide a kind of semiotic of the shared Edgeworth attitudes concerning what is valuable in education and what the appropriate response should be to the fundamental changes in society which they were enthusiastically endorsing.

Brian Hollingworth
30th August 2006.

Chapter Three

Saving Mrs. Mason's Soul: How Blake Rewrites Mary Wollstonecraft's *Original Stories from Real Life*

Amy Carol Reeves,
University of South Carolina

James McGavran, in his introduction to *Romanticism and Children's Literature in Nineteenth-Century England*, notes that, "Almost as old as Christianity itself was the debate as to whether Jesus suffered the little children to come unto him because of their innate goodness or their innate corruption."[1] These two views, both what McGavran has called the Romantic, idealized view of the child and the other view, a "powerful blend of Puritan Morality and John Locke's empirical psychology"[2] become ferociously juxtaposed in Mary Wollstonecraft's texts and William Blake's illustrations in the 1791 edition of *Original Stories from Real Life*.

As she tries to redeem her two young, irrational, and selfish nieces, Wollstonecraft's character, Mrs. Mason, resembles the matriarchal instructor found in so many late eighteenth- and early nineteenth-century didactic texts. Like Charlotte Smith's Mrs. Talbot, she is stern, rational and acutely sensitive to the injustices in her society. Because of her excessive perfectionism, and her distaste for passion, imagination, and fantasy, Romantic writers such as Blake, thought such a teacher essentially—soulless.[3] Though critics such as Orm Mitchell have shown

---

[1] McGavran, 1.
[2] Ibid., 5.
[3] Mitzi Myers provides a good history of the disdain among critics both during the Romantic period and in contemporary criticism towards these strict matriarchal instructors. One of the most bitter sentiment comes from the quote she provides from the modern critic Paul Hazard, "Let us flee….There is a whole battalion of

how William Blake's illustrations for the children's book are a critique of Mrs. Mason's severe lessons for her young wards,[4] Mary and Caroline, the illustrations are more than just a critique or parody. Rather, Blake offers an alternative vision of education—one in which the adult rather than the child experiences mental and emotional growth catalyzed through her experiences with children—a vision embodied well in his *Songs of Innocence and of Experience* in which his illuminations emphasize his belief in children as the means through which adults might understand spiritual matters. In Wollstonecraft's story, while the text tells the story of Mary and Caroline's increasing rationality and social awareness through their lessons with Mrs. Mason, Blake's six illustrations from plate 1 to plate 6, show the growth of Mrs. Mason's sympathetic nature. As he illustrates it, Blake is rewriting, not just critiquing, Wollstonecraft's story.

Plate 1 foreshadows Blake's revision, for he introduces Mary and Caroline as morally superior to their governess, while, at the same time, shows their desire to elevate her to their spiritual understanding. Plate 2 is a metaphor for Mrs. Mason's spiritual distance from childhood sensibilities of empathy and feeling. Plate 3 shows Mrs. Mason as divorced from sympathetic feeling when confronted with poverty and despair. Plate 4 shows Mary and Caroline leading Mrs. Mason towards the point of her redemption. The climax of Blake's counter story occurs in plate 5, as Mrs. Mason sees a vision of the child as a divine being. Finally, plate 6 shows a life transformed as Mrs. Mason enters into Mary and Caroline's world and can thus *feel* the pain of others.

First, in plate 1, Blake reverses Wollstonecraft's depiction of Mary and Caroline as morally inferior to Mrs. Mason. In her introduction to the book, Wollstonecraft tells us that when Mrs. Mason comes to instruct the girls, Mary and Caroline were:

> shamefully ignorant, considering that Mary had been fourteen, and Caroline twelve years into the world. If they had been merely ignorant, the task would not have appeared so arduous; but they had caught every prejudice that the vulgar casually instill. In order to eradicate these prejudices, and substitute good habits instead of those they had carelessly contracted, Mrs. Mason never suffered them to be out of her sight …. They had tolerable capacities; but Mary had a turn for ridicule, and Caroline was vain in her person.[5]

---

these fearsome women: Hannah More, Mary Wollstonecraft, who undertook to transform young girls into essentially rational creatures." Myers, "Impeccable Governesses, Rational Dames, and Moral Mothers," 41.
[4] Mitchell, "Blake's Subversive Illustrations," 17-34.
[5] Wollstonecraft, *Original Stories from Real Life,* vii-viii.

In addition to Wollstonecraft's dire assessment of Mary and Caroline's character, the first chapter opens with Mary and Caroline participating in the "cruel" game of smashing and destroying insects,[6] Mrs. Mason realizes that her first task is to teach the girls how to respect the natural world that "a good and wise God has created."[7] Wollstonecraft's Mrs. Mason, evidently, is more intimate with this God than the "ignorant" and "cruel" girls. But Blake, who might have known that children read pictures more avidly than texts, begins *his* counter story in the frontispiece which depicts Mrs. Mason, rather than the girls, as in need of spiritual and moral salvation.[8]

The frontispiece, more than any of the other plates, is the one most open to critical misunderstanding. Specifically, a 1799 French edition of *Original Stories* published every plate except this one. Though G.E. Bentley is the first to point this out,[9] he claims that he "can form no persuasive conjecture as to why [the publisher] Dentu or [the translator] Lallemant chose to omit it beyond parsimoniousness."[10] However, the fact that the title drastically changed from *Original Stories from Real Life; with Conversations Calculated to Regulate the Affections, and Form the Mind to Truth and Goodness* to simply *Marie et Caroline,* implies the editors' wish to refocus attention on the child characters and deemphasize Wollstonecraft's intent to reshape and regulate her wards' minds and affections. The frontispiece, they might have thought, would overly showcase Mrs. Mason's moral superiority. This view is also supported by Bentley's important observations that the editors omitted certain, "preachy" segments, specifically "some theological passages,"[11] and that the translator made subtle but essential word changes such as equating "happiness with pleasure."[12]

Recent critics such as Pfau, when he views plate 1 as a *critique* of Wollstonecraft's texts through comparing it with "Nurse's Song" in *Songs of Experience,* underestimates the plate's defiance of the textual story.[13]

---

[6] Ibid., 2.
[7] Ibid., 3.
[8] Blake, in a letter to Dr. Trusler, claims that children "have taken a greater delight in contemplating [his] Pictures" than he ever hoped. Blake to Dr. Trusler, 23 August 1799, 9.
[9] Bentley, "Marie [sic] Vollstoncraft [sic] Godwin and William Blake in France," 125-47.
[10] Ibid., 126.
[11] Ibid., 128.
[12] Ibid.
[13] Thomas Pfau, "'Positive Infamy,'" 220-42.

Pfau claims that the frontispiece of *Original Stories* shares the similar purpose of Blake's "Nurse's Song" which he claims is "a shrewd critique of pedagogical practice."[14] But Blake's frontispiece here goes much further than his later illustration for "Nurse's Song." He is beginning his own story purposed towards overthrowing what Wollstonecraft has set up in her introduction—Mary and Caroline's "shamefully ignorant" minds and dispositions and Mrs. Mason's inherent ability to eradicate their "vulgarities."

"Nurse's Song" from *Songs of Experience* depicts the nurse as lording over two children—one kneels in the background while the other stares straight ahead, not resisting his nurse's efforts to groom his hair. Though Mrs. Mason, like the Nurse, appears to lord over her wards, standing above them with arms outstretched as a Christ figure, an examination of the faces and positioning of Mary and Caroline shows that her iconic position derives from self-deception. Far from vulgar and in need of Mrs. Mason's offered "salvation," Mary and Caroline, unlike the children in "Nurse's Song," stand empowered, both morally and spiritually. The girls' hats suggest halos, while Mrs. Mason's large hat seems worldly and functional—she wears an attire more fit for Georgian era mothers and wives rather than for cherubs and angels.[15] Their gazes are upward, towards the heavenly and spiritual, while Mrs. Mason's is downward, symbolizing her limited vision and preoccupation with "lowly" concerns. Furthermore, while the children in "Nurse's Song" stand *within* the doorway, as if confined by their Nurse away from the fruitful, blossoming vines outside the doorway, in this frontispiece, the vines rise almost above Mary and Caroline's heads. Empowering the children in plate 1 enables Blake to better contest Wollstonecraft's notion of Mrs. Mason as the moral/spiritual saviour of children, while providing us with a vibrant introduction to his pictorial counter story of Mrs. Mason's spiritual impoverishment and her nieces' ability and willingness to "save" her.

Plate 2 depicts "crazy Robin," the poor man from Mrs. Mason's past, who, amid poverty, suffered the death of his wife, his children, and, finally, his beloved dog, carelessly shot by a young gentleman. The illustration shows Robin standing, with his fists clenched over the bed of

---

[14] Ibid., 232.

[15] Mitchell in "Blake's Subversive Illustration" has noted the blatant functional nature of Mrs. Mason's hat in the pictures. Regarding the frontispiece, he states that, "Mrs. Mason wears a large cumbrous bonnet" the "children's halo-like hats" (25). Furthermore, regarding plate 4, he notes, "In the illustration Mrs. Mason is again wearing a large Puritan-type hat (a reference perhaps to the puritan tradition of using fear to coerce the child into behaving)" (29).

his two dead children, Jacky and Nancy, with his dog at his side. Blake's choice of subject in this plate seems odd, because Mrs. Mason's purpose for telling the story is to teach Mary and Caroline about why they should always treat animals kindly. Indeed the inscription under the plate states, "The Dog strove to attract his attention.—He said: 'Thou wilt not leave me!'" But the *children,* not the *dog,* are the focus of this illustration. The children lie illuminated, looking heavenward while Robin, the adult, looks downward at the children. The adult's gaze and the children's gazes seem to mimic the gazes of Mrs. Mason and the girls in plate 1; the adult's focus is on the earthly while the children's in on the heavenly. Plate 2, indeed, seems to be a darker version of plate 1. Everything surrounding the adult embodies darkness and imprisonment: he is shrouded in darkness with black walls behind him and a darkened window shadowed with bars. The children, on the other hand, are enveloped in light, with peaceful faces, very different from the adult's grieving one. The children's state of death, in which they are separated from the adult, both physically and spiritually, symbolizes the vast distance between the adult's reality and the child's reality. The children exist in a spiritually vibrant, heavenly world, while the adult remains entrapped in an earthly "hell" of frustration and pain. Particularly, when compared with plate 1, plate 2 can be read as a metaphor for the emotional/spiritual distance between Mrs. Mason's view of reality and that of her two wards.

This plate cannot be about the barriers death imposes between the living and their deceased loved ones, because Blake refused to recognize such barriers. To William Hayley, Blake wrote:

> I know that our deceased friends are more really with us than when they were apparent to our mortal part. Thirteen years ago I lost a brother & with his spirit I converse daily & hourly in the Spirit & See him in my remembrance in the regions of my Imagination. I hear his advice & even now write from his Dictate. Forgive me for Expressing to you my Enthusiasm which I wish all to partake of Since it is to me a Source of Immortal Joy: even in this world by it I am the companion of Angels.[16]

Thus, the agony Robin must be facing is his inability to attain the spiritually enlightened state in which Jacky and Nancy exist. His torment lies in the fact that he stands too much in the "dark," (quite blatant in the plate), too much enmeshed in the cares of the earthly world to see how ubiquitous the spiritual world is. Because of this, he cannot converse with or be "the companion of Angels" and he represents Mrs. Mason's

---

[16] Blake to William Hayley, 6 May 1800, 15-16.

spiritually void existence. Plate 3 further emphasizes the distance between the sensibility of the adult and that of the child and explicitly shows how Mrs. Mason is divorced from childhood sensibilities of feeling and empathy. In the text, Mrs. Mason, Caroline and Mary visit the former sailor Jack and his wife and children. Jack tells them the details of his sorrows—the tragedies he experienced at sea and the poverty he and his family live in at home. Wollstonecraft portrays Mrs. Mason as entirely sympathetic. Jack tells the children:

> "I might now have been begging about the streets, but for [Mrs. Mason]"....
> A tear strayed down Mrs. Mason's cheek, while a smile of benevolence lighted up her countenance.[17]

Although the text portrays Mrs. Mason as sympathetic, in Blake's illustration, both Mrs. Mason and Jack are strangely placid.

This illustration is disturbing at several levels. The room, as in plate 2, is extremely dark. While Caroline and Mary, along with Jack's children, weep bitterly, Mrs. Mason smiles distantly while Jack stares ahead, statue-like. Welch describes well the detached nature of both adults:

> [Jack and Mrs. Mason] sit back unresponsive to the children's distress. The governess watches her charges calmly, her hands not even turned up in support of them as they cry in her lap. Jack is even less supportive as he sits stiffly with his hands in his lap, looking at Mrs. Mason, ignoring Mary's, Caroline's, and his family's sorrow.[18]

As Welch points out, children in this picture are the only feeling beings. Only the children weep over their shared sorrows.

So far, in Blake's counter story, plates 1, 2, and 3 show the adult's emotional distance from the sympathetic nature of children. Beginning with plate 4, Blake depicts the first move towards Mrs. Mason's redemption from her soulless, unfeeling state. In this plate, Mary and Caroline lead Mrs. Mason towards redemption, towards the point of epiphany, where she comes to develop the sympathy and spiritual enlightenment of her young wards.

In order to teach the girls about the dangers of procrastination, in Wollstonecraft's texts, Mrs. Mason leads them to the ruined estate of Charles Townley. There she tells them about how Townley's

---

[17] Wollstonecraft, 74.
[18] Welch, "Blake's Response," 10.

procrastination led to his own ruin, as well as to the ruin of those whom he loved best. Even though they hesitate, Mrs. Mason leads the girls towards the ruined house. Unlike any other part of *Original Stories*, Wollstonecraft takes great care to describe the intricate details of the crumbling estate:

> Ivy grew over the substantial walls, that still resisted the depredations of time, and almost concealed a noble arch, on which maimed lions couched; and vultures and eagles, who had lost their wings, seemed to rest for ever there. Near it was a rookery, and the rooks lived safe in the high trees, whose trunks were all covered with ivy or moss, and a number of funguses grew out of their larger roots.[19]

Mrs. Mason's urgency to show them the dilapidated grounds and the girls' hesitation at approaching the mansion (Mrs. Mason notices that Mary "trembles") indicates that Mrs. Mason is showing them the potential "ruin" that awaits them if they do not desist from harmful behaviours such as procrastination. The exterior corruption of Townley's house symbolizes his own "corruption," as well as the internal moral corruption taking over Mary and Caroline hearts, if they do not correct their errors.

Blake's illustration tells a different story. Instead of Mrs. Mason leading Mary and Caroline to a point at which they might realize their errors and lead more moral lives, it is *Mary and Caroline* who are leading Mrs. Mason. One of the girls has her arm behind Mrs. Mason as if urging *her* forward. Also, as in the frontispiece, the girls are wearing their halo-like hats. Interestingly, Mrs. Mason's gaze remains focused ahead of them, while only one of the girls looks forward while the other looks behind. This would seem to indicate that Mary and Caroline have extra vision, which Mrs. Mason does not have, what Blake would call double, threefold, or fourfold vision.

In one of Blake's letters to his patron, Thomas Butts, he writes some verses he composed while walking on a path to meet his sister, a walk in which he describes his double, threefold, and fourfold vision. In lines 28-30 he exclaims "double the vision my Eyes do see, / And a double vision is always with me." Later in the poem he disparages those who see only the material, those who approach everything with only rational minds. He states:

> Now I a fourfold vision see,
> And a fourfold vision is given to me;
> 'Tis fourfold in my supreme delight

---

[19] Wollstonecraft, 83.

And threefold in soft Beulah's night
And twofold Always. May God us keep
From Single vision & Newton's sleep![20]

Newton, Blake believed, simplified everything into the material and allowed for nothing spiritual or divine on earth. Avoiding "Newton's Sleep," for Blake, means maintaining more than single vision; it means seeing the spiritual as well as the earthly.

Here, in plate 4, Mary and Caroline, who, like Blake, have the ability to simultaneously see the spiritual and earthly, urge Mrs. Mason to walk with them. Like the cherubs in Blake's frontispiece to *Songs of Innocence and Experience*, they lead Mrs. Mason forward into a more spiritually and morally enlightened state, one in which she, like them, will not be limited by single vision.

This plate foreshadows plate 5, the climax of Blake's pictorial story, and the point at which Mrs. Mason experiences her dramatic moment of "salvation." According to Wollstonecraft's text, Mrs. Mason is walking amid the ruins of a Welsh castle, rather than amid the ruins of Townley's estate. But if we read Blake's picture as a separate story, she is in the place to which Mary and Caroline were leading her in plate 4. In Wollstonecraft's texts, amid these Welsh ruins at night, Mrs. Mason comes upon a hut, where she finds:

> an old man, [sits] by a few loose sticks, which blazed on the hearth; ... The man had been playing on the harp, he rose when he saw me, and offered me his chain.[21]

Blake takes full liberty with his illustration of this text. Instead of depicting an old man playing a harp, he presents a boy playing a harp, illuminated in blazing light. Blake portrays the old Welsh harp player as a child-angel. Mrs. Mason approaches the child with reverence and awe, her hands slightly tense, in joyful surprise. At this moment in Blake's revised story, Mrs. Mason sees the child, rather than the adult, as an enlightened being. She sees the child's spiritual nature and his capacity for feeling in utmost glory. She is, at the moment, "saved"—she is no longer "soulless."

Though other critics such as Orm Mitchell have noted how Blake's illustrated harpist, unlike the harpist in Wollstonecraft's text, has a youthful appearance and embodies imaginative potential, Mitchell calls

---

[20] Blake to Thomas Butts, 22 Nov. 1802, 46.
[21] Wollstonecraft, 115.

him "a young virile Welsh bard in creative ecstasy,"[22] plate 5 possesses greater implications for Blake's story. The harpist is not just a youthful creative bard, but a child-saviour. That Mrs. Mason here has a conversion experience, a moment of spiritual salvation in which she sees the child, rather than herself, as the true possessor of spiritual authority, is supported by Blake's poem, "The Lamb," in which the child, God, and the Lamb (or Christ) all stand connected:

> He is called by thy name,
> For he calls himself a Lamb:
> He is meek & he is mild,
> He became a little child:
> I a child & thou a lamb,
> We are all called by his name.[23]

Unlike Mrs. Mason in the frontispiece, in plate 5, the child as saviour is "meek" and "mild," sheltered among the castle ruins on a starry night. The plate has striking visual parallels to biblical images of the birth of Christ in a stable under a sky illuminated by angels and the star of Bethlehem. Though amid humble surroundings, the child-saviour seems to burst with divine energy, beaming light throughout his poor shelter. Mrs. Mason approaches the child-saviour as she would a divine being, head bowed and hands pointed out, prayerful and worshipful in appearance. But Mitchell has interpreted this plate as showing Mrs. Mason's stubborn resistance to spiritual vision. He states:

> the harper is the active force attempting to put Mrs. Mason in the way of imaginative vision. But if she is one the verge of opening her mental world through the inspired music of the young Welsh bard, she hesitates.[24]

Mitchell's interpretation, however, does not connect plate 5 with the plates before or following it. By understanding all the plates as a counter story, we see plate 4 as depicting Mary and Caroline as active agents in bringing about Mrs. Mason's epiphany in plate 5. Moreover, plate 6 shows us that plate 5 was, indeed, a moment of redemption.

In the final illustration, plate 6, we see how Mrs. Mason, when confronted with the misery of others, responds differently than she had in

---

[22] Mitchell, 29.
[23] Blake, "The Lamb," lines 13-18.
[24] Mitchell, 29.

plate 3. When visiting London, Mrs. Mason takes the girls to the home of a poor family, whose children felt the burden of poverty:

> The gaiety natural to their age, did not animate their eyes, half sunk in their sockets; and, instead of smiles, premature wrinkles had found a place in their lengthened visages. Life was nipped in the bud; shut up as it began to unfold itself.[25]

Mary and Caroline *and* Mrs. Mason, in this sixth plate, unlike the one in which they visited Jack, empathize completely with the poverty of the family. Mrs. Mason's face here exhibits all of the intense sadness that her young wards express, as she sees the suffering in the room. Mrs. Mason's sympathetic nature, in this conclusion to Blake's story, has matured through her relationship with Mary and Caroline. *She,* rather than the girls was, in need of redemption. As children, they were the catalysts for her moral salvation.

Blake's visual portrayal thus operates as a pictorial story constructed to counter Wollstonecraft's tale. He is going further than simply *critiquing* it; he is rewriting her text. Furthermore, it obscures Blake's fury regarding what he saw as adults' limiting and derogatory views of children to read his plates as mere critiques. As the illustrator of *Original Stories,* Blake could not bear to leave Mrs. Mason as he felt Wollstonecraft had left her, self-righteous and spiritually void. Eight years after illustrating and revising Wollstonecraft's story, Blake was going to illustrate the works of another writer, Dr. John Trusler. Unfortunately, Trusler felt as if Blake was lived too much in "the World of Spirits." To him Blake wrote, "I am really sorry that you are fall'n out with the Spiritual World."[26] Later, after defending his position that the world is one of imagination, vision, and spiritual sensation, he writes:

> But I am happy to find a Great Majority of Fellow Mortals who can Elucidate My Visions & Particularly they have been Elucidated by Children who have taken a greater delight in contemplating my Pictures than I even hoped. Neither Youth nor Childhood is Folly or Incapacity. Some Children are Fools & so are some Old Men. But There is a vast Majority on the side of Imagination or Spiritual Sensation.[27]

Blake believed that the fictitious Mrs. Mason was not the only adult in need of saving. Those adults who regarded youth and childhood as "folly

---

[25] Wollstonecraft, 172.
[26] Blake to Trusler, 8.
[27] Ibid., 9.

or incapacity," adults such as Trusler, and indeed Wollstonecraft, adults whom Blake saw as "fall'n out with the Spiritual World," were to him, in a dire and grievous state. The pictorial story he inserts as a counter text in Wollstonecraft's work represents, most certainly, his vision of the possibility for salvation for the unwavering, single vision, rationalists of the world.

Did Wollstonecraft know how much Blake subverted her story? If so, what did she think? Though solid evidence regarding their relationship is sketchy, Blake and Wollstonecraft almost certainly knew each other. Because Blake not only illustrated *Original Stories*, but likely also engraved some of the plates for Wollstonecraft's translation of G.C. Salzmann's *Elements of Morality, for the use of Children,* the authors may well have corresponded. As Bentley has suggested, both worked so closely with Joseph Johnson (Wollstonecraft even living with him for a period) that they probably met at his literary dinners. Furthermore, Blake's poem "Mary" may well reflect upon Mary Wollstonecraft and his *Vision of the Daughters of Albion* seems to have been influenced by her writings. [28]

With this evidence in mind, if both children's writers did indeed meet at literary dinners any debate in their writings likely mirrored real, actual debates arising in Johnson's circle. Wollstonecraft, herself, might not have been surprised that the fiery and controversial Blake would counter her story in this way. The fact that such a prolific and liberal-minded writer as Wollstonecraft never directly opposed Blake in her writings suggests that, she may have approved of the 1791edition of *Original Stories,* subversion and all. Such an edition of the book would have put forth the debate itself as a testimony to the ongoing and evolving conversation about the nature and role of the child. Such a view of *Original Stories* opens up new possibilities for interpreting this book for children. Specifically, the book presents itself as a fierce *debate* rather than just a fiercely *moral story.* Geoffrey Summerfield, the modern children's literature critic and author of *Fantasy and Reason* writes:

> *Original Stories* has a strong claim to be the most sinister, ugly, overbearing book for children ever published. It is permeated by a grim, humourless, tyrannical spirit of hectoring and unswerving spiritual and mental rectitude—all in the name of healthy growth: a dream of reason producing, indeed, a veritable monster in the form of Mrs. Mason, the book's equivalent of Day's Barlow and Trimmer's Mrs. Benson. "I will give you a moral for your dream," writes Lady Fenn in 1789; but Mrs. Mason, relentless, severe, preoccupied with the "regulation of appetites" in

---

[28] Bentley, " 'A Different Face,' " 349.

her two young charges, Mary and Caroline, gives them morals for their waking nightmares.[29]

Many critics of Wollstonecraft's book share Summerfield's sentiments. But an examination of Blake's pictorial counter-story along with Wollstonecraft's textual story reveals *Original Stories* to be a vibrant debate, rich in portraying radical and varied opinions regarding the nature of the child, issues of authority between adults and children, and finally, issues of pedagogical structure—whether the power to "teach" lies in the realm of the adult or the child.

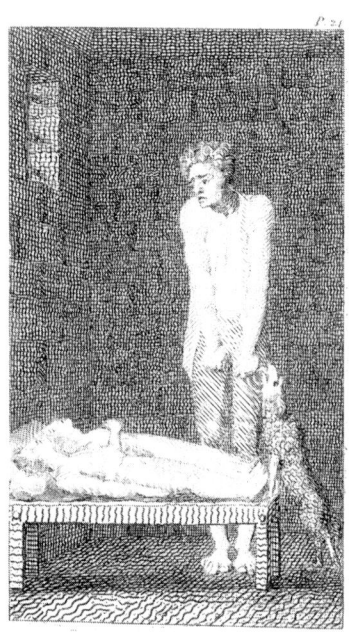

Fig. 1. (Beinecke Rare Book and Manuscript Library, Yale University).

Fig. 2. (Beinecke Rare Book and Manuscript Library, Yale University).

---

[29] Summerfield, *Fantasy and Reason,* 229.

Saving Mrs. Mason's Soul: How Blake Rewrites Mary Wollstonecraft's 49
Original Stories from Real Life

Fig. 3. (Beinecke Rare Book and Manuscript Library, Yale University).

Fig. 4. (Beinecke Rare Book and Manuscript Library, Yale University).

50   Chapter Three

Trying to trace the sound, I discovered a little hut, rudely built.

Œconomy & Self denial are necessary in every station, to enable us to be generous.

Fig. 5. (Beinecke Rare Book and Manuscript Library, Yale University).

Fig. 6. (Beinecke Rare Book and Manuscript Library, Yale University).

List of Illustrations

Fig. 1. William Blake, Plate 1, 1791. New Haven: Beinecke Rare Book and Manuscript Library, Yale University.

Fig. 2. William Blake, Plate 2, 1791. New Haven: Beinecke Rare Book and Manuscript Library, Yale University.

Fig. 3. William Blake, Plate 3, 1791. New Haven: Beinecke Rare Book and Manuscript Library, Yale University.

Fig. 4. William Blake, Plate 4, 1791. New Haven: Beinecke Rare Book and Manuscript Library, Yale University.

Fig. 5. William Blake, Plate 5, 1791. New Haven: Beinecke Rare Book and Manuscript Library, Yale University.
Fig. 6. William Blake, Plate 6, 1791. New Haven: Beinecke Rare Book and Manuscript Library, Yale University.

Works Cited

Ackroyd, Peter. *Blake.* New York: Alfred A. Knopf, 1996.
Bentley, G.E. "Marie Vollstonecraft Godwin and William Blake in France: The First Foreign Engravings after Blake Designs." *Australian Journal of French Studies.* 26 (1989): 125-147.
—. "'A Different Face': William Blake and Mary Wollstonecraft." *Wordsworth Circle.* 10 (4) 1979: 349-50.
Blake, William. *The Letters of William Blake.* 3rd ed. Ed. Geoffrey Keynes. Oxford: Clarendon Press, 1980.
—. *Songs of Innocence and of Experience.* Ed. Geoffrey Keynes. New York: The Orion Press, 1967.
Chandler, Anne. "Wollstonecraft's *Original Stories*: Animal Objects and the Subject of Fiction." *The Eighteenth-Century Novel.* 2 (2002): 325-51.
McGavran, Jr. James Holt, ed. *Romanticism and Children's Literature in Nineteenth-Century England.* Athens: The University of Georgia Press, 1991.
Mitchell, Orm. "Blake's Subversive Illustrations to Wollstonecraft's *Stories.*" *Mosaic: A Journal for the Interdisciplinary Study of Literature.* 17 (1984): 17-34.
Myers, Mitzi. "Impeccable Governesses, Rational Dames, and Moral Mothers." *Children's Literature.* 14 (1986): 31-59.
Pfau, Thomas. " 'Positive Infamy': Surveillance, Ascendancy, and Pedagogy in Andrew Bell and Mary Wollstonecraft." *Romanticism.* 2 (1996): 220-42.
Pinheiron de Sousa, Alcinda. "Is There a 'New Woman' in Mary Wollstonecraft's *Original Stories* as Illustrated by William Blake?" *The Crossroads of Gender and Century Endings.* Ed. Alcinda Pinheiro de Sousa, Luisa Maria Flora, and Teresa de Ataíde Malafaia. Lisbon: Colibri, 2000. 7-20.
Summerfield, Geoffrey. *Fantasy and Reason.* London: Methuen, 1984.
Welch, Dennis M. "Blake's Response to Wollstonecraft's *Original Stories.*" *Blake: an Illustrated Quarterly.* 13 (1979): 4-15.

Wollstonecraft, Mary. *Original Stories from Real Life; with Conversations, Calculated to Regulate the Affections, and Form the Mind to Truth and Goodness.* 1791. Otley: Woodstock Books, 2001.

Chapter Four

Matrilineal Descent: Mother, Daughter and the Seeking Soul in Mary Shelley's *Proserpine*

Carolyn A. Weber, Seattle University

> I saw the King of Hell in his black car,
> And in his arms he bore your fairest child,
> Fair as the moon encircled by the night, –
> But that she strove, and cast her arms aloft,
> And cried, "My mother!" – [1]

In the winter of 1820, while the Shelleys were residing in Pisa, Mary Shelley began working on two mythological dramas, *Proserpine* and *Midas*. Over a century later, Sylva Norman condemned Mary Shelley's plays as unworthy of "analytical and comparative study."[2] When they have been considered noteworthy, it is usually for their short inset verses by Percy Bysshe Shelley. Oddly dismissive for a first editor, Elizabeth Nitchie, who discovered the 1832 publication of *Proserpine*, writes that *Proserpine* and *Midas* are "distinguished only by the lyrics that Shelley wrote for them."[3] Nitchie joins a long tradition of ignoring Mary's verse in favour of Percy Bysshe's. After an entire chapter on Percy Bysshe Shelley, Douglas Bush, for instance, assigns Mary merely a paragraph in his next chapter, "Nineteenth Century Minor Poets," claiming that *Proserpine* and *Midas* "are not important, but they enable us to read

---

[1] Arethusa tells Ceres of Proserpine's abduction in Mary Shelley's drama *Proserpine. A Drama in Two Acts*, Act II, lines 73-77. All references to the drama are taken from Pamela Clemit's edition in volume 2, pp. 73-82 of *The Novels and Selected Works of Mary Shelley*.
[2] Norman, 98.
[3] Nitchie, 157.

Shelley's lovely lyrics in the setting for which they were designed."[4] Percy Bysshe would repeatedly eclipse Mary, the "moon" of his *Epipsychidion*.[5] Even with the recent increase in Mary Shelley criticism, however, the dramas themselves remain relatively overlooked. For instance, while Charles Robinson's extensive work on Mary Shelley lends her dramas more serious attention, his main reasons for doing so still remain primarily relative to Percy Bysshe.[6] Only very few contemporary critics, such as Marjean Purinton and Julie Carlson, have begun to address *Proserpine* as a fascinating work in its own right in more sophisticated ways, extending their discussions to include the drama's treatment of sexual identity and patriarchal/matriarchal systems.[7]

This oversight is unfortunate, given what a rich text Mary Shelley's *Proserpine* offers in the study of parent-child constructions and their sociopolitical (as well as spiritual) ramifications during the Romantic period. First, Mary Shelley creates in her drama a metaphorical discourse between mother and daughter that is at once highly personal and yet mythically universal. She draws on the established notion of the Proserpine story as an allegory for the soul's journey and renders it particular to the soul journey of the female artist. Highly sensitive to having been born of her mother's death – a fact that colours her work as well as her own construction of herself throughout her lifetime – Mary would naturally be attracted to a myth with metempsychosal undertones, or the passing of souls from one body into another, seen, for example, in the conflation of mother and daughter. In her adaptation of Ovid's myth, Mary emphasises a "common soul" among all women (but especially those who dare to write in a man's sphere) that defies the fragmentation seemingly initially imposed upon them by a patriarchal dictate. Second, *Proserpine* offers a rare example of Romantic drama composed by a woman with a female audience in mind, especially a young and formative female audience, given its topographical construction as a drama for children. Mary's choice of genre here is a strategic one, as it literally gives voice to the plight of women–daughters and mothers–involving the authorship of their own lives.

Grace Stewart examines in depth the sources for a woman's sense of identity, and the influence of the mother on a daughter's artistic

---

[4] Bush, 171.
[5] See Dunn's discussion of Mary's construction of herself in *Moon in Eclipse: A Life of Mary Shelley*.
[6] See Robinson's introduction in his edition of *Mythological Dramas: Proserpine and Midas, Bodleian MS. Shelley d.2.*
[7] Carlson, 351-72; Purinton, 385-411.

development. She claims that young girls tend to internalise a concept of mothering as the equivalent of womanhood, and that society encourages that tendency.[8] A deep connection between mothers and daughters exists that is physical as well as emotional, intellectual and spiritual:

> From her mother or on her own, [a woman] learns her potential power – awesome not only to others but to herself as well. She experiences physical changes – menses, pregnancy, childbirth, lactation, and menopause – all of which magically transforme her relations with others but also affect her, without control. She learns seductive powers that can transform a man physically but can unleash a male force destructive to her body and spirit. On the other hand, she learns or senses that her own seductive power must not overwhelm her lover lest she appear unfeminine and terrify him. Women learn from men, as well as from their mothers, that to be feminine is to be selfless and to nurture.[9]

The simultaneous feelings of power and weakness related to her body often betray themselves in a woman's imaginative expressions and constructions. As Stewart examines, if the establishment of identity is difficult and central for any woman, then the problem must be acute for the female artist. For, if to be female is "to mother," then to be an artist, devoted to self-expression, is to be unfeminine. This, of course, forms a fundamental issue behind *Frankenstein*. But the physical and philosophical conflicts find counterparts within the female artist's highly self-conscious approach to construction, even of herself as "artist." In their discussion of identity and the female artist, Carol Pearson and Katherine Pope explain "Unlike the male artist ... the female artist faces internal conflicts between the selfless role of the heroine and the self-expressive role of the artist."[10]

Proserpine's story offers a perfect mythological medium for exploring and setting forth such issues surrounding the female artist. Particularly when we set them against the metempsychosal relationship that Mary Shelley builds between herself and her mother, Mary Wollstonecraft, the myth of Proserpine becomes a loaded choice for a dramatised subject on Mary Shelley's part. As Stewart summarises, "Indeed, the myth of Demeter/Persephone crystallises the mother/daughter cathexis and the

---

[8] Stewart, 128.
[9] Ibid., 129.
[10] Carol Pearson and Katherine Pope, eds., 194-5. Dorothy Dinnerstein (1976) emphasises that a woman's relationships with men do not sever her associations with her mother, but they can confuse the "focus of her mirror-image."

mysteries related to that relationship."[11] *Proserpine* testifies to Mary Shelley's interest in the feminine artistic soul-journey, as conveyed through a mother-daughter discourse.

The Myth of Proserpine as Female Soul Journey

On 3 May 1820, Mary records finishing *Proserpine*, which was later published in the *Winter's Wreath* for 1832, accredited to "the Author of Frankenstein."[12] It was not published separately until André Koszul's edition of the two dramas in 1922. Written on the heels of her novella *Matilda*, the subject matter remains similar: loss and searching, the division or "sharing" of the soul between mother and daughter, the invasion of the male (paternal/lover) figure, the interweaving of death and life in allegorical soul journeying. But in her adaptation of the myth of Proserpine, Mary Shelley returns to the mother figure with full force. Here mother and daughter become more conflated than ever before as Mary Shelley strives to convey the feminine spiritual and artistic experience through myth.

Classical notions about Proserpine and Ceres come to us through such texts as Homer's epics, Apollodorus's writings, Hesiod's *Theogony* and Ovid's *Metamorphoses*. According to Graeco-Roman mythology, Proserpine, the only child of Jupiter and Ceres, (all also known by the names Persephone/Kore, Jove/Zeus, and Demeter, respectively) became goddess of the Underworld after her abduction by Hades (Pluto, Tartarus, or "Death"). An unwilling victim torn from her mother, she must – under the patriarchal rule of the male gods – spend part of the year (usually seen as half or a third) with her "husband" in hell. During the remaining months, she may inhabit the earth in reunion with her mother. Consequently, Ceres, in her anger and her mourning, ceases the earth's fertility in her daughter's absence. The myth has been used to express the division of the seasons, and was celebrated in many rites shared by mother and daughter, notably the Eleusinian mysteries and the Thesmophoria. In these rituals, Proserpine's name was not spoken, except, perhaps, at the secret ceremonies reserved for initiates. She was referred to simply as Kore (Maiden). Overall, however, she is a complex character. As the ruling goddess of the Underworld, she is often depicted as more powerful or influential in controlling the activities of the spirits of the dead or dying

---

[11] Stewart, 130.
[12] *Journals of Mary Wollstonecraft Shelley*, 316 (henceforth referred to as *MWSJ*).

than Hades himself.[13] Furthermore, she represents the spirit of the world's dying and reviving vegetation.

The specific mother-daughter association of Ceres and Proserpine with women's experience is a rich and ancient one. Historically in Greek civilization, the Demeter-Kore legend (according to the mythic Greek names) embodied the central cultic myth of two primary and famous celebrations of femininity. In the Greek world, one was the Thesmophoria, an Athenian ritual festival held exclusively by and for women. The other formeed the Eleusinian mysteries, thought to be originally an "Earth-mother fertility religion," involving only women and administered by priestesses. Among the divinities of ancient Athens, it was this mother-daughter pair "most often invoked by women, who alone swore by the 'twain goddesses.'"[14] The Romans continued the worship of the mother-daughter mythic pair according to the names of Ceres and Proserpine, whose story was ritually re-enacted by Roman matrons and virgins.[15] The Shelleys, who were great readers of classical history and literature, surely were aware of such associations and rituals.[16]

"Metempsychosal" Readings of the Tale

In Book V of his *Metamorphoses*, Ovid provides the oldest known recorded source for the Proserpine myth. Mary Shelley read Ovid's work throughout the spring of 1815, and returned to it again almost to the day five years later, about the time she was writing her own version of the Proserpine tale.[17] Because of its recurring presence and importance in the Shelleys' reading, Ovid's epic deserves some historical consideration, especially as it pertains to the metempsychosal. The *Metamorphoses* shows Ovid's handling of the epic to be complex: it is both celebratory and subversive. Ovid's *Metamorphoses* is essentially metempsychosal: not only are the stories that comprise the overall work repeatedly based upon the transference of souls into other bodies (humans usually become beasts

---

[13] Proserpine's sway over Pluto is apparent in the story of Orpheus and Eurydice; cf. Virgil's *Georgics* and Ovid's *Metamorphoses*.
[14] Keuls, 64, 112, and 351-53; see also Tyrell (1984), 69-71.
[15] Pomeroy, 216-17.
[16] The classical sources for such history, which the Shelleys did or may have read or been familiar with, are too numerous to mention. One example lies in the works of Aristophanes, which the Shelleys record reading in the early summer of 1818; *MWSJ*, 633. The women of *Lysistrata*, for instance, repeatedly refer to following such cults.
[17] *MWS Journals*, 665.

as punishment, or are immortalised as a reward, by the gods), but Ovid's technique emphasises the ceaseless and inter-dependent pairing of creation/destruction. His epic proves that "all things change, yet never die."[18] Thus Ovid has the "philosopher" of the final book claim:

> Nothing retains the shape of what it was,
> And Nature, always making old things new,
> Proves nothing dies within the universe,
> But takes another being in new formes.
> What is called birth is change from what we were,
> And death the shape of being left behind.
> Though all things melt or grow from here to there,
> Yet the same balance of the world remains.[19]

Whether regarding mortality, the natural world, science or spirituality, everything feeds back into itself, its identity transferred and transformed.

Regarding Ovid's final overt assertion of his work's overall theme, Horace Gregory explains:

> As [Ovid] came to the last of his fifteen books, he felt the need of a philosophy to sustain his device of eternal transformations. An Alexandrian Greek philosopher, a certain Sotion, had recently come to Rome. He was a disciple of Pythagoras, a vegetarian, and a popular lecturer. Ovid incorporated the gist of his lectures into Book XV. The Pythagorean doctrine with its protest against the killing of animals made its appeal to the human warmth of Ovid's character, and it allowed him to give a semblance of Lucretian seriousness to his entire work. Ovid's nature of things was the nature of transformations. *He did his best to make Pythagorean theory support the large design of The Metamorphoses.* He had rounded out his conception of a world he had promised to reveal in Book I. However shallow many of Ovid's convictions were, he held to his belief that nothing in the world could be destroyed; all things become transformed – and not least, his own poetry into an immortality.[20]

This link between Ovid and Pythagoras is an important one within the context of my discussion of *Proserpine*. The Romantic and prolific translator, Thomas Taylor, whose editions were standard and readily available to the Shelley circle, asserts that the main myth celebrated in the *Mysteries of Eleusis* is the story of the descent of Proserpine into Hades,

---

[18] Ovid, *Metamorphoses*, 419.
[19] Ibid., 421.
[20] *Metamorphoses*, Introduction by Horace Gregory, pp. xxv-xxvi (emphasis mine).

and the search of her Mother, Ceres, for the lost child. Taylor interprets this myth in the tradition of the later Platonists, taking the Virgin Proserpine as the (feminine) soul descending into generation. Taylor cites Apuleius as one authority for understanding the myth of Proserpine as an account of the descent of the soul into incarnation. Given Mary Shelley's translation of the Psyche myth from Apuleius in 1817, we begin to see just how interlinked her texts and interests of 1817-20 were, especially with her overt emphasis on mythic heroines of the soul's journey during these two years. Pluto "signifies the whole of material nature," and the cavern provides "the entrance, as it were, into the profundities of such a nature;" hence Proserpine's "rape" by Pluto manifests the soul's "union with the dark tenement of the body." Taylor continues to explain that the tale of Proserpine is a "divine fable" showing the two-fold state of the soul:

> one part of which is supermundane, subsisting with Jupiter, or the Demiurgus, and together with him establishing one artificer of divisible natures; but the other is mundane, in which Proserpine is said to be ravished by Pluto, and to animate the extremities of the universe. "Hence," says Proclus, "according to the rumour of Theologists, who delivered to us the most holy Eleusinian mysteries, Proserpine abides on high, in those dwellings of her mother which she prepared for her in inaccessible places, exempt from the sensible world. But she likewise dwells beneath with Pluto, administering terrestrial concerns, governing the recesses of the earth, supplying life to the extremities of the universe, and imparting soul to beings which are of themselves inanimate and dead.[21]

The Proserpine story acts as an ancient allegory for the recurring descent and ascent of the soul. This would have been a plausible and imaginatively attractive interpretation available to the Romantics.

Kathleen Raine offers a fascinating thesis on Blake's reworking of the myths and editorial ideas found in Taylor's *Commentaries of Proclus* and *Eleusinian Mysteries* that is applicable to several themes found in Mary Shelley's work:

> There is already a psychological element in the Neoplatonic interpretations of the theme of the Soul's descent. Plotinus wrote that "the whole soul does not enter the body, but something belonging to it always abides in the intelligible, and something different in the sensible world." The relation of Persephone to Ceres is, on one level, psychological; and the relation between the unconscious sleeping generated part of the soul, to the all-knowing eternal part, may well have given Blake the first

---

[21] Taylor, *A Dissertation on the Eleusinian and Bacchic Mysteries,* 455.

suggestion of themes that he later made his own – the relation between the spectral selfhood and the eternal humanity, the Imagination ....

> Thus understood, we may pause to admire the wisdom of the Neoplatonic myth (for to say the old Mysteries of Eleusis really held this meaning is a different matter) by which the Mother seeks the Child; it is the eternal that seeks the temporal, the divine that seeks the human, as the vision seeks the visionary.[22]

Themes common to Mary Shelley and the myth include the importance of parent-child relations, the "search" or "pursuit," and the wayward child (*Frankenstein* and *Matilda* immediately come to mind). Then there is the role of the female visionary through prophetess-like figures, dreams and foreboding. The influence of such a pertinent myth as that of Proserpine warrants closer examination in relation to Mary Shelley's work.

Feminist Readings of the Tale

The modern feminist poet Adrienne Rich calls the Proserpine myth "the essential female tragedy," which involves the "loss of the daughter to the mother, the mother to the daughter."[23] Similarly, Marylin Arthur looks at the insistence upon male superiority that joins with hostility toward the "female principle" in ancient literature.[24] She remarks, "it might seem as if we would look in vain for positive or sympathetic expressions of female consciousness." But, aside from the existent fragments of a few female poets, Arthur claims "there are some other works of Greek literature and art which, upon analysis, reveal a peculiarly feminine sensibility." She names one of these as the Homeric Hymn to Demeter, or the story of the rape of Proserpine, because it "treats the transition from 'matriarchy' to 'patriarchy' from the female point of view, and therefore takes the forme of a series of attempts to resist male domination rather than to impose it." Arthur continues:

> The hymn, as I see it, could be subtitled "how to be a Mother goddess in a Patriarchal Society," since the central problematic of the poem is Demeter's search for recognition and identity in a male-dominated cosmos. On one level Demeter's plight is therefore that of all women, who must struggle to achieve self-definition in a social and psychic world which values male attributes more highly and depreciates females.

---

[22] Raine, 41-3.
[23] Rich, 237.
[24] Arthur, 8.

Arthur's argument takes us to the issue of female alienation within a male "cosmos:" in particular, a male established and propelled artistic discourse. Indeed, Mary Shelley most likely perceived herself as alone with her mythology in cultural terms, for gendered interpretations of the Ceres/Proserpine myth such as Arthur's holds parallels with women's alienation from learning in general, and their abduction into a "man's world" when in fact this learning takes place. Richardson speculates that Mary Shelley's interest in classical authors at the time that she was working on these mythological dramas "might be taken as her asserting a claim on the classical tradition considered in her age and place as the exclusive heritage of upper-class males." Richardson compares Mary Shelley with Keats, seeing her as "essentially self-educated" and "an outcast from the British system of classical education, belatedly approaching the Greek myths via Ovid."[25] But unlike Keats, Mary Shelley, as a woman surrounded by literary men, and writing for/against her late literary mother, finds a mythology such as that of Ceres/Proserpine to be a particularly relevant one as a personal and political organising metaphor.

In this way, Mary Shelley's attraction to metempsychosis, and her use of it as a medium for both aesthetic and spiritual exploration of the female (writing) experience holds significant repercussions for understanding constructs of Romanticism, as well as their subsequent feminist offshoots. The Ceres/Proserpine motif has grown increasingly attractive to feminists as an organizing metaphor for female experience. While it has always been essentially a "feminine" myth, as discussed earlier in terms of its rites and significance to women of the ancient world, it must be said that Mary Shelley's appropriation of it for distinct socio-artistic ends was precocious. Mary Shelley's turning to and treatment of the Proserpine tale offers a precursor of the tale's popularity among such later women writers as Elizabeth Browning, Virginia Woolf, Adrienne Rich, Margaret Atwood, Jeanette Winterson and Eavan Boland. These writers use the myth as a structural metaphor in their representation of the female artistic experience. Susan Gubar argues that the myth becomes an allusive structure in so much of women's poetry because it articulates the pain of growing up female in a male-dominated world: "For Shelley, the myth of Ceres and Proserpine is a female version of *Paradise Lost* in which the original gold-ripe garden is lost not through any female sin, but because of the interference of a man."[26] While Mary Shelley may have entertained nostalgia for a fading gender-based social system of etiquette (arguably

---

[25] Richardson, 127.
[26] Gubar, 303-5.

seen, for instance, in *Valperga*), or a preoccupation with engendered power structures, her handling of the myth also displays an attempt to transcend the finite with the personal experience. As her Proserpine asks, "can immortals weep?/ And can a Goddess die as mortals do,/ Or live & reign where it is death to be?".[27]

In *Proserpine*, Mary Shelley writes herself into the text as "daughter," and so, as journeying "soul," or the developing feminine principle. She casts the Wollstonecraftian wise mother-figure as Ceres. Susan Gubar compares Ceres to the sphinx, while, as discussed earlier regarding *Matilda*, Taylor identifies Ceres as "the self-inspective part of our nature, which we properly denominate intellect," and Proserpine "the vital, self-moving and animating part which we call Soul." Syndy Conger writes that "If Ceres represents Mary Shelley's wish-fulfilment fantasy of a living, loving, and supportive, yet courageously defiant, mother, Proserpine is most certainly her as a daughter.[28] How telling that Mary Shelley would construct an understanding of immortality through the metaphorical relationship of the daughter as soul and the mother as (undying) intellect. The motif conveys the cycle Mary Shelley felt a part of in relation to her mother, and the circles in which she felt trapped as a female writer in her time. But the same construction also expresses the eternality of the soul journey which balances the personal with the transcendent, the earthly with the ethereal. *Proserpine* provides a variant to this motif found throughout the writings of the Romantic period.

Mary Shelley's Appropriation of Proserpine

Traditionally, Mary Shelley's drama has been dismissed as merely a reworking of Ovidian myth for a younger audience.[29] Though Robinson still calls it an adaptation from Ovid's *Metamorphoses*, at least he notes the revisions and variations that make *Proserpine* a "more adult" narrative.[30] More perceptively, Richardson notes how: "*Proserpine* and *Midas* are of great interest on several fronts: as a woman writer's innovative assault on classical mythology; as generic experiments; and as unusual collaborative ventures which raise questions regarding the differences between female and male approaches to poetic invention in the

---

[27] *Proserpine*, 88.
[28] Conger, 95.
[29] See, eg., Bush, 171. de Palacio primarily sees the plays as providing categorical evidence of Mary Shelley's continuing interest in Latin and Greek, 564-71.
[30] Robinson, 13-14.

early nineteenth century."[31] In her introduction to the dramas, Clemit claims, "Mary Shelley's choice of episodes from Ovid further suggests that the plays were designed for a young audience." But then, importantly, she adds, "in *Proserpine*, she adapts the tale of the rape of Proserpine by Pluto to focus on the interaction between Proserpine and her mother Ceres."[32] None of these critics, however, examine the mother-daughter relationship further.

But Mary Shelley's rendering of the myth betrays significant differences, both marked and subtle, from its Ovidian source. In *Proserpine*, she shows how the act of writing itself connects daughter to mother, both personally and politically.[33] Her subject allows her to engage in a transmigrational type of discourse with her late mother, where the "souls" of the women become interchangeable, their stories intertwined, while her choice of genre politicises the plight of the female writer. Mary Shelley was drawn to the story of Proserpine, just as she was drawn to that of Psyche, because of the symbolic soul journey subtexts to the myth, and its specific emphasis on rendering this through a central mother-daughter relationship.

Mary Shelley's *Proserpine* greets its audience with an extremely mother-directed opening. The deviation from Ovid is immediate and twofold. On one level, the purely narrative, story-establishing level, Mary Shelley sets up her young heroine as preoccupied with her mother. Proserpine fears separation from her, and begs her "Go not, dear Mother, from your Proserpine." Mary Shelley winds Proserpine about Ceres just as the daughter weaves a chaplet for her mother's hair. But on another level, Mary Shelley begins her metempsychosal discourse with her own mother. The opening language suggests Wollstonecraft's "The Cave of Fancy" with Proserpine's first words:

> Dear Mother, leave me not! I love to rest
> Under the shadow of that hanging cave
> And listen to your tales.[34]

Mary Shelley engages simultaneously in telling an "objective" story *and* "talking" through the shared medium of writing to/with her own late mother. Symbolically, she opens her play in the landscape of the maternal,

---

[31] Richardson, 124.
[32] See Clemit's note to *Proserpine*, 70.
[33] Interestingly, Conger sees *Proserpine* as a revisiting of Wollstonecraft's *Maria*; "Mary Shelley's Women in Prison," 94.
[34] *Proserpine*, 73.

with the daughter wanting to hear stories from her mother. Nowhere in Ovid's text does there occur any mention of a cave, or such a request from Proserpine. The scene illustrates daughters in narrative exchange with their absent mothers, a theme that runs throughout Mary Shelley's early work.

Within this opening scene involving daughter and mother, Mary Shelley takes liberties in adding details symbolically alien to Ovid's tale. For instance, Ovid does not draw attention to Ceres's abandonment of Proserpine, nor her hesitation to leave her daughter. Rather, the rape scene traditionally occurs quickly, after we read of the judgement passed by Jove, and the shaft from Cupid that pierced Death's heart. But Mary Shelley has Ceres articulate her greatest fear for her daughter as "You might be lost."[35] Being "lost," the state in which Mary Shelley's other heroine Mathilda most refers herself, has a double meaning, and the author, I believe, articulates the archetypal mother's greatest fear carefully. For while Proserpine might simply become geographically lost if she wanders too far away, she may also, and more dangerously, become "lost" to herself. Sexuality comes into it, but insofar as another coded metaphor for the greater "fall" of losing oneself, followed by the spiritual seeking thereafter of one's former state. Proserpine responds by wanting to hear the story of Prometheus, but then (perhaps in reproach of Percy Bysshe Shelley) she requests "the more pleasing tale of Aphrodite," the woman born from Ocean's foam who becomes immortal.

Mary Shelley continues to reinforce Proserpine's attachment to her mother in a way that smacks of her own life. Proserpine, for example, tells Ino "well I know the love you bear/ My dearest Mother prompts your partial voice,/ And that love makes you doubly dear to me." In other words, Proserpine is saying "You are dear to me because you loved my mother" – a sentiment that Mary Shelley held towards those who praised her own mother.[36] Mary Shelley prolongs the innocence, and the impending dread, with a long catalogue on the plucking of flowers. But she chooses not to show the actual rape, the central disturbing image in Ovid's version, complete with torn dress and dropped flowers. Instead, it is related to Ceres later by Arethusa. By omitting Ovid's directness, Mary Shelley maintains a state of decency for her fallen heroine. As in the case of her depiction of Psyche's "rape," Mary's "puritanical" editing could

---

[35] Ibid., 74.
[36] "The memory of my Mother has always been the pride & delight of my life; & the admiration of others for her, has been the cause of most of the happiness I have enjoyed," writes Mary Shelley a few years later to Frances Wright, 12 September 1827, *The Letters of Mary Wollstonecraft Shelley*, vol. 2, p. 3.

also be seen as protective. Her choices imply an act of solidarity with her heroine, and all "fallen" women. This latter interpretation seems more likely when read against the rest of the text. By keeping intact a veil of mystery surrounding the main event, Mary Shelley underscores a sense of inclusion among women in their community of communication.

In another example, nowhere does Ovid refer to the moon during the mid-day rape scene. Yet, at the height of the drama, Mary Shelley's Arethusa tells Ceres how she saw "the King of Hell in his black car, / And in his arms he bore your fairest child,/ Fair as the moon encircled by the night – ".[37] Given Mary's personal mythic connections to the moon, as well as its metempsychosal symbolism, such subtle liberties with Ovid's story tell us how Mary Shelley weaves herself throughout the tale in identification with the daughter specifically, and the female experience at large.

Mary Shelley has Ceres search the "wild wood" for her lost daughter. Ovid marks this in passing, but Mary Shelley reiterates it. Woods and vegetation, or *silva*, have already been established as ancient metempsychosal symbols for materialism. Ovid includes this setting, but Mary Shelley's greater emphasis on the woodland underscores that Proserpine has indeed "fallen." Mary's addition of "dreary caverns" highlights the fertility/fatality paradox, or the "womb/tomb" dichotomy, of her mythicised landscape. Significantly, Mary Shelley stages the reunion of Proserpine and Ceres, and the tension between masculine and feminine forces, over the threshold of a cave. These are images Mary Shelley has used deftly before in her metempsychosal play with symbolism. Similarly, Mary Shelley chooses to emphasise the consequent thirst Ceres feels upon losing her child. Ceres's slip into mortality as represented by such a mortal weakness as thirst occurs with the separation of her daughter from herself. Mary Shelley retains this detail from Ovid, but develops it by making it the focus of Ceres's first speech when she appears after searching for her daughter. Furthermore, when she blights the land at the loss of her daughter, Mary has Ceres act not out of grief, but rage. She renders Ceres an active, potent figure capable of bestowing both life and death. Mary Shelley takes Ovid's story as one based on the mother-daughter mythological relationship, and approaches it as worthy of political as well as personal consequence at this time in her life.

Mary Shelley's most significant digression from Ovid's text, however, is to give Proserpine an identity of her own. She achieved a similar character with Psyche, giving depth to the archetypal girl-figure by

---

[37] *Proserpine*, 85.

making her thoughtful, as well as highly empathetic. Mary Shelley's rendering of these young heroines as individualised, thoughtful beings grants them a closer identification with the Intellect as a spiritual symbol. This act recalls connections of the soul with "intellect" in metempsychosis theory, which extends, as discussed earlier, to the highly intellectualised spiritual relationship that Mary Shelley holds with her mother. Mary Shelley's concern with rendering her mother-daughter mythic heroines as overtly self-reflective, if not highly intellectual beings (Psyche, Proserpine, Diotima, Mathilda, for example), not only legitimises them in a masculine discourse based upon the validity of reason and "learning," but it also slides them well into ancient associations with the soul. As their author, she calls for their intellectual and spiritual validation.

Ceres's intellectual abilities should also be noted. In Ovid's tale, she succumbs to Jove's final judgement with relative resignation; Mary Shelley's Ceres, however, argues her position articulately and forcefully. She expostulates convincingly and relentlessly against Jove's unfairness. The final exchange results in a finale of mother-daughter eloquence in which their spiritual relationship overcomes any earthly separation forced upon them. The feminine rhetoric undoes the male judgement, as mother and daughter rejoin on a spiritual, imaginative plane. After Jove's final decree that Proserpine must return to be queen of Hades for half the year because she ate of its fruit during her abduction, Mary Shelley has Proserpine turn to her mother and say:

> Dear Mother, let me kiss that tear which steals
> Down your pale cheek altered by care and grief.
> This is not misery; 'tis but a slight change
> From our happy lot. Six months with thee,
> Each moment freighted with an age of love:
> And the six short months in saddest Tartarus
> Shall pass in dreams of swift returning joy.
> Six months together we shall dwell on Earth,
> Six months in dreams we shall companions be,
> Jove's doom is void; we are forever joined.[38]

Proserpine's words are more than an optimistic balm by which to soothe her mother. Rather, she *reasons* their fractured state back into wholeness through an imaginative response that transcends their predicament. In fact, Proserpine's reasoning is so convincing that although Jove's judgement divides her year perfectly in half, she makes her time with her mother in

---

[38] Ibid., 90.

the upper-world seem longer and more substantial than that which she must spend in Hades. Proserpine's recourse, and so true immortalisation, lies in her ability to connect the intellect with emotion, empathy *and* the imagination. In this way, the mother and daughter "halves" of the soul "escape" male-dominated, or disrupted existence to a higher level of connection. Where before their lives were lived in the innocent fields of earthly Sicily, after the insertion and disruption of the male into their "world," the two feminine halves rejoin in the "hereafter" of the imagination. In this ethereal "fields of fancy" of their minds, they find the afterlife of the intellect, the realm of souls.

Ceres's response to her daughter's imaginative reasoning also combines the intellectual with the empathetic, forming the speech on which the play ends. I quote Mary Shelley's version of the entire speech because of its terrible importance:

> Oh, fairest child! Sweet summer visitor!
> Thy looks cheer me, so shall they cheer this land
> Which I will fly, though gone. Nor seed of grass,
> Or corn shall grow, thou absent from the earth;
> But all shall lie beneath in hateful night
> Until at thy return, the fresh green springs,
> The fields are covered o'er with summer plants.
> And when thou goest the heavy grain will droop
> And die under my frown, scattering the seeds,
> That will not reappear till your return.
> Farewel, sweet child, Queen of the nether world,
> There shine as chaste Diana's silver car
> Islanded in the deep circumfluous night.
> Giver of fruits! For such thou shalt be styled,
> Sweet Prophetess of Summer, coming forth
> From the slant shadow of the wintry earth,
> In thy car drawn by snowy-breasted swallows!
> Another kiss, & then again farewell!
> Winter in losing thee has lost its all,
> And will be doubly, bare, & hoar, & drear,
> Its bleak winds whistling o'er the cold pinched ground
> Which neither flower or grass will decorate.
> And as my tears fall first, so shall the trees
> Shed their changed leaves upon your six months tomb.
> The clouded air will hide from Phoebus' eye
> The dreadful change your absence operates.
> Thus has black Pluto changed the reign of Jove,
> He seizes half the Earth when he takes thee.

Two distinctly metempsychosal reactions arise from Ceres's speech that support Mary Shelley's illustration of the myth as a female-centred soul allegory. The first appears in her cyclical language of death and resurrection. She explains how the natural world will mirror the loss of her daughter and her return, with Mary Shelley repeating such words as "return" and "reappear," along with "goest," "losing" and "lost" throughout Ceres's speech. Ceres refers to her daughter's absence in Hades as her "six months tomb," and imposes death on the world by vowing to have the earth sleep during this absence. Secondly, Mary Shelley demonstrates her metempsychosal framework by having the two female halves, mother and daughter, come fully together by the end of the play. Ceres's final speech openly expresses just that. Mother and daughter are immediately conflated as Ceres transfers her role unto her daughter. She opens her reply by calling Proserpine "sweet summer visitor," the name by which Ceres herself will become identified as a result of her curse. Daughter becomes mother as the queen of the harvest hails Proserpine "Giver of fruits!". Ceres also crowns her "Sweet Prophetess of Summer," an interesting detail given the importance Mary Shelley attaches to prophetess figures as literary resurrections of her own mother. Mother and daughter merge together more vitally than ever before in light of new knowledge of their division, followed by a mutual determination to transcend it imaginatively.

Thus, the final scene of Mary Shelley's *Proserpine* is one of triumph for the mythic female(s). Both mother and daughter declare Jove's judgement inconsequential. Just as Proserpine was de-flowered physically by Pluto, causing a literal division between mother and daughter, so Jupiter is de-powered imaginatively by the proposed transcendence of Proserpine. Separation – call it division, the Fall, emanation or generation – marks the fragmentation of the soul, and so its materiality and relative weakness. But mother/daughter reject this imposed separation by refusing to accept it. They each enter an imaginative contract to remain joined in spite of their sentence of physical separation. Proserpine's last words in the play end in a declaration to her mother, "Jove's doom is void; we are forever joined." Ceres echoes this in agreement, adding first her plan for solidarity with her daughter, and then its result in her curse (a winter worse than winter) upon Jove's kingdom. Mary Shelley ends the final scene with Ceres's resounding words: "Thus has black Pluto changed the reign of Jove,/ He seizes half the Earth when he takes thee." For Mary Shelley, a female "ethics of care" triumphs over a male "ethics of justice." Her play ends by emphasising that Jove actually lost half of his domain, and therefore much of his "earthly" power, through Proserpine's marriage.

Female unity – expressed in Proserpine's imaginative union with her mother, and by Ceres's determination to die with her daughter, and bring all of nature with her – wins out, so that the daughter extends into the mother and vice versa. Divided and yet one, the female soul is in an eternal state of flux, caught in a cycle of death and resurrection, but ultimately, reunion, and therefore, ethereally undefeatable, and so, immortal.

Voicing Daughters: Maternal Legacy and Community

Often major concepts in Romantic criticism remain tethered to a discussion of traditionally canonical male Romantic writers such as Blake, Percy Bysshe Shelley and Wordsworth. The same gender limitations occur in Alan Richardson's original advocacy almost two decades ago for a "mental theatre" as a means of understanding the transformation that took place in Romantic poetic drama.[39] It is not until his later article on Mary Shelley's dramas that Richardson widens his scope to include a female Romantic writer. But Mary Shelley proves problematic. The work of the fore-mentioned men all fit so nicely together in Richardson's theoretical application of Byron's term in attributing an "internalised" forme of poetic drama to the Romantics. However, while Mary Shelley's plays loosely fits the criteria of mental theatre, there exists an irony and a sympathy that makes her work relevant to the genre and yet a square peg in the round hole. In his article, Richardson senses this belonging and yet not-belonging: "lyrical drama, or 'mental theatre,' with its emphasis on character over plot, on reaction over action, and its turn away from the theatre is the genre to which *Proserpine* and *Midas* most nearly belong."[40] His comment that her plays "most nearly belong" suggests that they do "not quite" fit into this masculine category; instead, they remain a disturbing presence.

In his discussion of Wordsworth's *Borderers* as an example of mental theatre, Richardson argues for a pattern of "seduction and repetition" as it "arises from a Romantic conception of consciousness, and on how such a conception can best be approximated." But the pattern Mary Shelley emphasises is one of *abduction and repetition*. Richardson bases his definitions on a masculine understanding in which the very fact that the

---

[39] Richardson, *A Mental Theater: Poetic Drama and Consciousness in the Romantic Age* (1988).
[40] Richardson, "*Proserpine* and *Midas*: Gender, Genre, and Mythic Revisionism in Mary Shelley's Dramas," *The Other Mary Shelley*, 125.

protagonist is a "seducer" or "tempter" allows for free will, or an act of conscious choice, on behalf of the other (male) hero. But as Mary Shelley shows in the mental theatre of a Romantic female writer, there is no seducer or tempter, only a rapist. There is no choice or will on behalf of the (necessarily female) heroine. Rather, the situation of her utter powerlessness brings about the problematic nature of victimisation as associated with the socialised female condition. Yet, Mary Shelley portrays the female as ultimately powerful through the act of female communion. This is most powerfully portrayed at the play's close. When Proserpine has received the judgement of Jove, which banishes her to the underworld for half the year, Mary Shelley dramatises the other female characters' determination to join her. To Proserpine's cry, "If fate decrees, can we resist? farewel!", Ceres replies, "Is there no help, great Jove? If she depart/ I will descend with her – ." Both Ino and Arethusa join in, with Ino announcing:

> We will all leave the light and go with thee,
> In hell thou shalt be girt by Heaven-born nymphs,
> Elysium shall be Enna,–

To which Arethusa immediately adds:

> I will sink down with thee; – my lily crown
> Shall bloom in erebus, portentous loss
> To Earth, which by degrees will fade & fall
> In envy of our happier lot in Hell; –
> And the bright sun and the fresh winds of heaven
> Shall light its depths and fan its stagnant air.

The women of Mary Shelley's rendition of *Proserpine* determine to make their punishment their bliss. In many ways, they take control of an affliction that seems beyond their control, and the author highlights their togetherness in doing so. Their actions have metempsychosal repercussions. They reject an imposed degradation of the common female soul, opting instead to immortalise it through the "successful" community of women.

As the women of the play are rendered more and more physically helpless, they communicate with each other at higher and higher levels. One of the most important overall revisions that Mary Shelley applies to Ovid's tale is that she conceives it as a drama. That is, her version arises from the dramatic mode, from being *spoken*, from the authority of *voice*.[41] In and of itself, then, Mary Shelley's choice of genre sets up her revision of the myth as immediately political. The women dominate the stage. As Richardson points out, "the rapist-god Pluto and his brother, the Olympian patriarch Jupiter, remain offstage throughout." With the exception of one male character, Ascalaphus (the one who betrays Proserpine), all of Mary Shelley's characters in her rendition of Ovid's myth are women. The play consists solely and significantly of women's voices – women losing themselves in male-imposed individuality and finding themselves in community. As Richardson writes, *Proserpine* is "concerned with male tyranny, both that of Pluto and of the father-god Jove, but here the dramatic emphasis is placed on the community of women – goddesses, nymphs, and naiads – victimised by patriarchal tyranny and eventually united against it." He continues: "Where Ovid's version of the myth confirms the male pantheon's ascendancy, and blandly presents rape as an Olympian prerogative, Shelley's version restores something of Demeter's pre-Olympian power as Earth goddess, translated into the ethical and political force of women united as a community."[42] This female community functions on different principles than those of the "male domain." Richardson claims that what makes Mary Shelley's play so unique occurs because "Discursive exchange in *Proserpine* is based not, as is usual in drama, on conflict, but on empathy." *Proserpine* is so unusual precisely because Mary Shelley intended it to be. Her play offers a revisionist dramatization of women's voices expressing their ability to transcend fragmentation initially imposed upon them by patriarchal structures. The result is a celebration of the metempsychosal, and so "immortalizing" relationship, between mothers and daughters across generations.

Works Cited

Arthur, Marylin. "Politics and Pomegranates: An Interpretation of the Homeric Hymn to Demeter," *Arethusa*, 10. 1 (spring 1977): 7-47.
Bush, Douglas. *Mythology and the Romantic Tradition in English Poetry*. Cambridge. Mass.: Harvard University Press, 1937.
Carlson, Julie. "Coming After: Shelley's Proserpine," *Texas Studies in Literature and Language* 41.4 (winter 1999): 351-72.

---

[41] For eg., Daphne, Io and Calisto are female victims from Ovid's *Metamorphoses* who lose their voice.
[42] Richardson, "*Proserpine* and *Midas*," 128-30.

Conger, Syndy. "Mary Shelley's Women in Prison," *Iconoclastic Departures: Mary Shelley after Frankenstein*. London: Associated University Presses, 1997. 81-97.
de Palacio, Jean. "Mary Shelley's Latin Studies," *Revue de litterature comparée* 38 (1964): 564-71.
Dinnerstein, Dorothy. *The Mermaid and the Minotaur: Sexual Arrangements and Human Malaise*. New York: Harper and Row, 1976.
Dunn, Jane. *Moon in Eclipse: A Life of Mary Shelley*. New York: St. Martin's Press; London: Weidenfeld and Nicolson, 1978.
Gubar, Susan "Mother, maiden and the marriage of death: Women writers and an ancient myth," *Women's Studies* 9. 3 (1979): 301-315.
Keuls, Eva C. *The Reign of the Phallus: Sexual Politics in Ancient Athens*. New York: Harper and Row, 1985.
Nitchie, Elizabeth. *Mary Shelley: Author of "Frankenstein"* (New Brunswick: Rutgers University Press, 1953) 157
Norman, Sylva. "Mary Shelley: Novelist and Dramatist," *On Shelley*. London: Oxford University Press, 1938.
Ovid, *Metamorphoses*. Trans. Horace Gregory. New York: Penguin, 1960.
Pearson, Carol and Katherine Pope, eds. *Who Am I This Time?: Female Portraits in British and American Literature*. New York: McGraw-Hill, 1976.
Pomeroy, Sarah B. *Goddesses, Whores, Wives, and Slaves: Women in Classical Antiquity*. New York: Schocken, 1975.
Purinton, Marjean. "Polysexualities and Romantic Generations in Mary Shelley's Mythological Dramas *Midas* and *Proserpine*," *Women's Writing* 6.3 (1999): 385-411.
Raine, Kathleen "The Little Girl Lost and Found and The Lapsed Soul," *The Divine Vision: Studies in the Poetry and Art of William Blake*, ed. Vivian De Sola Pinto. London: Victor Gollanez, 1957.
Rich, Adrienne. *Of Woman Born: Motherhood as Experience and Institution*. New York: W. W. Norton, 1976.
Richardson, Alan. *A Mental Theater: Poetic Drama and Consciousness in the Romantic Age*. University Park and London, Pennsylvania State University Press, 1988.
Richardson, Alan. "*Proserpine* and *Midas*: Gender, Genre, and Mythic Revisionism in Mary Shelley's Dramas," *The Other Mary Shelley: Beyond* Frankenstein. Eds. Audry Fisch et al. New York: Oxford University Press, 1993. 124-139.
Robinson, Charles, Ed. Introduction. *Mythological Dramas: Proserpine and Midas, Bodleian MS. Shelley d.2.,* vol. 10, *The Bodleian Shelley*

Manuscripts, 10 vols. New York and London: Garland Publishing, 1992.

Shelley, Mary. *The Journals of Mary Shelley: 1814-1844*, eds. Paula R. Feldman and Diana Scott-Kilvert. Baltimore and London: Johns Hopkins University Press, 1995.

—. *The Letters of Mary Wollstonecraft Shelley*, ed. Betty T. Bennett, 3 vols. Baltimore and London: Johns Hopkins University Press, 1980.

—. *The Novels and Selected Works of Mary Shelley*, gen. eds. Nora Crook with Pamela Clemit; consulting ed. Betty Bennett, 8 vols. London: Pickering and Chatto, 1996.

—. *Proserpine. A Drama in Two Acts*. Ed. Pamela Clemit. Volume 2, pp. 73-82.

Stewart, Grace B. "Mother, daughter and the birth of the female artist," *Women's Studies* 6. 2 (1979): 127-145.

Taylor, Thomas. *A Dissertation on the Eleusinian and Bacchic Mysteries*. London, 1790.

Tyrell, William Blake. *Amazons: A Study in Athenian Mythmaking*. Baltimore: Johns Hopkins University Press, 1984.

CHAPTER FIVE

FAMILY SYSTEMS THEORY AND "THE MAN OF FIFTY YEARS" IN GOETHE'S *WILHELM MEISTER'S JOURNEYMAN YEARS*

INGRID BROSZEIT-RIEGER, OAKLAND UNIVERSITY

Troubled relationships that lead to experimentation with different family constructs appear as a common thread throughout Johann Wolfgang von Goethe's literary production.[1] Here, I will focus on the novella "The Man of Fifty Years," embedded in the novel *Wilhelm Meister's Journeyman Years or The Renunciants*, third in the *Meister* Trilogy and completed in its final version in 1829.[2] This novella plays out the dilemma of a closed, strictly self-reproductive family system to its final consequence, the threat of extinction.

The young woman Hilarie is supposed to marry her cousin Flavio to secure the unity and order of the family estate. Hilarie, however, is secretly in love with Flavio's father, her uncle, whereas Flavio is secretly in love with a so-called beautiful widow. The discussion of a drawing of the family tree reveals that Hilarie's love for her uncle is a displaced reproduction of her mother's youthful love for her brother, Flavio's father. If Hilarie loved Flavio under the parental conditions, she would replicate exactly the structure of her mother's desire and with the union of Flavio and Hilarie as the last links in the family tree, would integrate the family's emotional and economic riches into a closed system. The intrusion of Hilarie's unexpected love for her uncle into the parental plan, however, is only a distorted replication of her mother's desire and not a true alternative

---

[1] A feminist discussion of Goethe's problematic families, beginning with his early dramas, can be found in Hart, *Tragedy in Paradise*.
[2] Quotations refer to volume 10 of *Goethe: The Collected Works*.

to the established family dynamics. Nonetheless, this pathological triangle of affection provokes an evaluation of this closed self-sustaining family model and its impact on the identity of individuals dominated by the intent to preserve the status quo at all cost. In order to liberate the development of the self from damaging familial influences, Goethe introduces renunciation as a concept that dissolves family as a concrete, established reality by elevating it onto an ideational/idealistic realm.[3] This realm is only real in the thoughts and emotions of the individual because the renunciant agrees to go out into the world where s/he can communicate with family members only via correspondence. Thus, the individual is free of any limitations imposed by family home and relationships. Even though the novella seems to have an open ending due to Hilarie's insistence on renunciation, its main characters re-emerge later in the main text of the novel and resolve their conflicts.

This miniature family saga must surprise the reader considering the novella's title, because "The Man of Fifty Years" leads us to expect a middle-aged man's trials and tribulations. When we are presented with the perspectives of three main characters involved in the dilemma of love triangles and family survival, it seems ironic that the title only mentions the uncle. The irony lies in the fact that the novella focuses its attention on the relationship between its characters rather than on the perspective of only one character.[4] The discrepancy between the projection of the title and the development of the narrative exposes a character-focused view as

---

[3] As Arthur Henkel shows in *Entsagung:Eine Studie zu Goethes Altersroman* (Tübingen: Niemeyer, 1964), Goethe does not give a clear and comprehensive definition of "renunciation" in any of his writings. However, in her introduction to volume 10 of *Goethe. The Collected Works,* Jane Brown points out a general effect of "renunciation" that also explains the function of this concept for individuals in overpowering families: "By demonstrating the limits to our understanding and to our control of our passions and imagination, the novel preserves a realm beyond the reach of its oppressive social structures: this is the most important and positive aspect of renunciation" (8). Furthermore, in his monograph *The Novel As Archive*, Ehrhard Bahr defines the process of "renunciation" and its outcome as follows: "Goethe's idea of renunciation begins with sacrifice and develops into compensation for an unsatisfactory situation, resulting in a payoff on a different level" (26). In "The Man of Fifty Years," "rejection and sacrifice lead to a rearrangement of physical possession among the four individuals involved." (28). For the conception of renunciation in Goethe's writings see Ponzi, 150-59.

[4] In *Goethe's Cyclical Narratives*, Jane Brown observes increasing irony in the progression of the novella, 68 n.3. Other selective arguments on irony in the *Journeyman Years* are Ehrhard Bahr, (Berlin, 1972), Benjamin Bennett, (Cornell UP, 1993), and Clark Muenzer, (Pennsylvania State UP, 1984).

limiting. Instead, this discrepancy seems to suggest the importance of interpersonal relationships that shape a character's self-perception and behaviour. In order to pinpoint those factors that determine the inter- and intra- personal relationships of individuals, family systems theory offers a valuable theoretical framework. The differentiated terminology of this theory enables any analyst to unravel how a family or an individual is organized, how it functions, malfunctions, and may heal its pathological tendencies. "In systems thinking, in contrast to popular individualistic thinking, a person is not a freestanding, constant entity but achieves her or his nature of the moment through interaction,"[5] and so also do Goethe's characters in the novella. I have chosen *Metaphors of Family Systems Theory* by Paul C. Rosenblatt as my theoretical work of reference because this study summarizes and evaluates the body of research that defines the field of family systems theory. Even though this book is written for "professionals who specialize in studying or helping families [...] from a social constructionist perspective" (2) it also enhances the literary scholar's work of exposing complexities of the dynamics and implications of family relationships by adding a new psycho-social perspective to the established approaches to literature. First of all, Rosenblatt clarifies that "a family system consists of a set of people and their relationships with one another. What distinguishes systems thinking from the view of families taken in individual psychology is the emphasis on interaction processes, on the dynamics among the people in the system" (51) that is "not necessarily stable." (51) Rosenblatt's discussion of family systems theory includes a set of categories, for example, family as entity, structure and system, with the respective subcategories of family boundaries, system control, and communication patterns. These categories enable me to conceptualize the family in "The Man of Fifty Years" in terms of family dynamics, motivations, pathology, and recovery.

In using the term "metaphor" in his title, Rosenblatt implies a connection between family systems theory and literature by giving language a creative as well as self-reflective role. He emphasizes his intent to account for the phenomenon that the wording of a category or an observation shapes the way of how thinking about that same category or observation is organized by associations with other paradigmatic uses. Thus, metaphor is defined here in a broader than literary sense as a mental

---

[5] Rosenblatt, 59. See also Niklas Luhmann, *Love as Passion* (1982), for a connection between systems theory and the representation of social codes of intimacy in eighteenth-century literature.

tool for organizing one's reality.[6] The categorical metaphor that dominates the family in "The Man of Fifty Years," namely family as an entity, exemplifies how family metaphors pre-structure as well as censor thinking about family in terms of its qualities. Rosenblatt's elaboration applies in detail to our fictional family:

> The bias for family members and others to perceive the family as an entity sets goals for the family. These goals have to do with working toward a family with the characteristics of a group that can be perceived as an entity [...] through, for example, exclusive interaction, proximity, and shared experience. (37)

Therefore, "attention is drawn to the ways family members are similar [and] [...] attention will be drawn away from the ways family members are dissimilar, the large amount of time in which they do not interact together or are physically distant from each other [...]" (38) thus "obscuring [...] competition, difference, and disunity" (41).

The family in Goethe's novella appears from the very beginning as a self-contained, self-sufficient entity through its social superiority, aristocratic residence, genealogical relationships, and commitments and obligations of family members to each other. The characters' identity is first established by their high social rank, the uncle as "major," his sister as "baroness" and later on by their physical location in relation to their estate, either the house, the garden, the surrounding land or away from it. For example, when the major arrives at home after an apparently longer absence, the narrator underscores that "the major had ridden into the courtyard, and Hilarie, his niece, was already standing outside on the steps leading up to the manor house, waiting to receive him." (212-13) Location also determines the characters' demeanor and mode of expression. Outside, family members tend to express their thoughts and emotions rather freely and directly and in the case of the major's arrival with gestures of affection: "She [Hilarie] flew to him, he pressed her to his breast" (213). On the other hand, the interior of the manor house demands more ritualized behaviour and indirect expression such as "spirited and expressive playing" (213) of the piano or communicating through the exchange of poems or the pleasant arrangement or giving of objects to

---

[6] Rosenblatt bases his use of metaphor on the term in G. Lakoff and M. Johnson, *Metaphors We Live By* (Chicago: University of Chicago Press, 1980), namely that metaphor "saturates thought and is necessary for organizing and focusing thought but that it also obscures what is not within the reality defined by the metaphor currently being entertained" (Rosenblatt 3).

support a warm and caring atmosphere in the home.[7] Everyday routine, extra-ordinary activities as well as major decisions are all directed toward the general well being of the family unit. The plan of joining Hilarie and Flavio in marriage emerges in the parental generation as the strongest expression of the family's highest goal to secure and strengthen its unity and to increase its wealth, as a reflective moment in front of the family tree reveals:

> The major found his sister standing before the family tree, which she had had hung up, prompted by conversation the previous evening about various collateral relations, who, because they were unmarried, or had gone to live in distant lands, or had even totally disappeared, raised in greater or lesser degree the hope of large legacies either for brother and sister or for their children. They discussed the question for some time, without mentioning the fact that previously all family worries and endeavors had focused solely on their children. (221)

Thus, worries about the family's survival as a unit cause the major and the baroness to sacrifice their individuality for the sake of a family identity. The parents' loss of individuality and depreciation of selfhood become evident in the fact that they are never mentioned by name and that they expect their children to surrender their individuality to family goals as well. In desperation, the major pleads to his son transferring the whole burden of the family's anxiety onto his offspring:

> The entire agreement among the surviving members of our family rests on the assumption that you will be united with Hilarie. If she marries a stranger, then the whole fine and clever consolidation of a respectable fortune is shattered, and you especially will not be well provided for (223-24)

because the manor with surrounding land is Hilarie's inheritance from her deceased father who was "a large landowner and serious farmer" (236).

---

[7] In *Love as Passion*, Niklas Luhmann claims that love constitutes a code of communication that "encourages one to have the appropriate feelings" (9). In order to create intimacy, successful communication has to refer to a familiar "specific socio-cultural framework" (14) as well as include a "personal level" (14) of "differentiation" (17) conveying the intent of going "beyond the call of gallant duty" (23). Luhmann considers the act of "'giving'" (26) an essential part of the personalization of the code. On the other hand, for a valuable psychoanalytic reading on the exchange of poetry and other gifts see Y. A. Elsaghe, "'Helle' und 'Hölle:' Zur Rolle der Dichtung in *Wilhelm Meisters Wanderjahren*," *Goethe Yearbook* 7 (1994): 118-32.

The major's lack of parental sensitivity results from an exaggerated notion of family as an entity. Rosenblatt explains in general terms:

> The metaphor of the family as an entity leads people to think of the family as existing independently of its members. Once the family is defined as an independent entity, it can be thought of as having its own needs and a life of its own [...] and as something that can be benefited or harmed independently of its members. (36)

Even though Hilarie and Flavio rebel against their parents' matchmaking, they still show a deep-seated alignment with the family's self-definition to the outside in their role as strong, capable and benevolent patrons. A river marks the periphery of the family's estate and occurs as a natural boundary between the family and the outside world. When a flood threatens the safety of the estate's surrounding region, Hilarie and Flavio join in several rescue and care-giving missions to help flood victims, despite their fear of "lurking" (243) dangers. Above all, their contacts outside of the family are rare and generally associated with danger. Aside from a ball the baroness hosts, the family only receives one visitor, an old friend, an actor, whom major and baroness had not seen for a long time, emphasizing the social isolation of the family. Despite the joy over this reunion, both siblings associate their guest with danger and instability, as the narrator interjects the memory of the actor's risky affair with a "distinguished lady" in his youth from which the major and his sister rescued him "when he was threatened with a most sorry fate" (216). The other social contact to the outside world, whom Flavio and later also his father seek, is the beautiful widow and her circle. The women in the family, however, resent the "fair widow" (230) labeling her a "born coquette" keen on "attracting men and holding them fast" (231).

The family's fear of outside influences is especially linked to women, who enter the family circle and influence males through their emotional impact. Therefore, anxiety about change motivates the goal of keeping the family as closed, uniform, and unchanged as possible, as change seems to imply chaos and the possible destruction of the family from undermining forces on the inside. When Hilarie asks her uncle to explain the family tree to her, this anxiety resurfaces in the uncle's recollection of family history:

> The major began his account with the oldest ones. [...] Then he went on [...] observed that a grandfather often reemerged in a grandson, spoke [...] of the influence of the women, who, marrying in from other families, often altered the character of entire lines. [...] Finally he reached the

bottommost rows. There were his brother the marshal, himself and his sister, and beneath them his son, with Hilarie next to him (221)

as if the latters' future was unalterably inscribed into this chart with the purpose to ultimately protect the family from outside influences. Families that are particularly closed, such as the novella's, are considered "disturbed" (88) and "imply pathology" (88) according to Rosenblatt. Our fictional family illustrates how the pathological fear of foreign influence culminates in multiple unhealthy incestuous relationships under the guise of loyalty to the family.[8] The narrator summarizes:

> The baroness had loved her brother since childhood so much that she had thought of him superior to all other men, and perhaps even Hilarie's inclination had, if not sprung directly from this preference of her mother's, surely been fostered by it. All three were now joined in one love, one delight, and blissful hours sped by for them. (222)

With the same inappropriateness, the baroness "shared in" Hilarie's "bridal feeling" (237) while assembling her dowry.

To the same extent as boundaries to the outside are too closed, they are too open within the family. This unbalanced situation leads to enmeshment, a "pathological" (103) condition resulting from lacking differentiation and excessive cohesion. Rosenblatt explains:

> A family thought of as relatively cohesive might be characterized as having high levels of connectedness, physical togetherness, or emotional togetherness. The extreme of cohesiveness might be described as an undifferentiated family ego mass [as we have here], as a family that is emotionally fused or enmeshed, or as a family that has diffuse or blurred individual boundaries with very little tolerance for family members' autonomy. (102-103)

As a result of her enmeshment with her mother and cohesion with her family, Hilarie makes a commitment to her uncle promising "I am yours forever" (221) in front of the family tree as soon as she realizes that her

---

[8] Research on sibling relationships in Goethe's works has been focused on the brother-sister dynamics. Isolde Salisbury (1993) emphasizes the aesthetic function of the so-called symbolic brother-sister relationships for the maturation of the male sibling in all of Goethe's works, thus omitting the topic of sisterhood altogether. JoAnna Stephens Mink and Janet Doubler Ward (eds. 1993) take the diversity of sibling relationships and pertinent psychological literature into account, thereby offering a helpful model for further Goethe scholarship in this area.

family's survival is in jeopardy. Therefore, her rejection of Flavio is only a seemingly rebellious act because her choosing the uncle instead still supports the family goal of continuing the family in a closed fashion. Furthermore, being homebound and isolated from people outside her family, Hilarie's choices are extremely limited.[9] Later, when Hilarie betrays her promise to the uncle and pursues Flavio's affection in order to assume the place of the beautiful widow in the latter's heart, the circumstances resemble the situation in front of the family tree. After Flavio has returned home critically ill from grief over his rejection by the beautiful widow, he proclaims that his blood still "belongs to" the widow, "all of it" (239). In turn, Hilarie reacts corresponding to the family tree on behalf of the family entity, wanting to secure Flavio's blood for the continuation of the family, thus keeping the biological resources of the family contained within. Hilarie's outcry "The blood, the blood – it belongs to her, all to her, and she is not worthy of it" (239) underscores the impact the family metaphor of bood has on Hilarie's emotions. In her eyes, saving the bloodline, the life energy that is passed on from one generation to the next as the essence of a family, redeems her transference of affection from uncle to cousin. Furthermore, the conflicting motivations of enmeshment and family cohesion with the rebellious impulse against both cause Hilarie's internal dilemma of only painful choices, a situation that cannot be resolved without physical and emotional detachment and the establishment of healthy personality boundaries between her as a separate individual and her family.

Family structure and system control, however, preserve the family entity and support a high level of family cohesion and enmeshment, preventing any "flexibility for individual needs to be met" (Rosenblatt 103) on a self-developmental level while familial roles are restrictive and keep each member in a gridlock.[10] Everyday life progresses in a "rigid

---

[9] For details on the social and cultural history informing the novella see Herweg (1997).

[10] Rosenblatt defines family structure as follows: "The metaphor of family structure highlights the systematic arrangement of family members in terms of roles, interaction patterns, attachment relationships, and other perceivable, orderly, and at least somewhat enduring patterns" (98). Thus, the family system has an internal supra-structure that regulates the interplay of all categories and metaphors relevant for the organization and functioning of a family system in order to benefit the ultimate family goals. Furthermore, each family system has control mechanisms in place to keep the establish system in balance. "Control metaphors highlight regularity and regulation in family interaction. The rules metaphor highlights the possibility of unverbalized but effective family understandings" (6).

order" with "domestic rituals" (214) in which every member assumes a clearly defined role: the baroness supervises the general organization and appearance of the house. The uncle organizes and oversees matters of the family estate and finances, devoting "his waking hours to inspections and investigations" (231). Hilarie entertains the family with her piano playing and provides comfort and pleasantries for the male relatives when they return home, such as arranging the uncle's room "for his comfort in the old, familiar manner" (214). Flavio is expected to fill the role as his father's successor. Therefore, Flavio's resemblance to or difference from his father repeatedly becomes a focal point in the text, indicating a latent anxiety in the family of whether Flavio may be adequately fit to assume his father's position, since the "father was somewhat taller" and his coat "was rather too long" (241) for the son. [11] The fact that Flavio already follows the paternal example with his own military career and his patriarchal leadership in the rescue mission during the flood covers up this anxiety. While a superficial harmony embellishes the surface of role division, pleasant family interaction, and the symmetry of aunt, uncle, daughter, son, and female and male cousins, it unravels as soon as family members forme coalitions in pursuit of common interests. As a reaction to the parents' marriage plot, both children rebel by falling in love with someone else. When the baroness, here the supportive mother, reveals her daughter's romantic affection to her brother, the two siblings disagree about the "naturalness" and authenticity of Hilarie's feelings; the baroness finds it a "natural," the major an "unnatural" (214) inclination. Later on, when Hilarie becomes romantically involved with Flavio, the baroness keeps this new development from her brother. In this way she transforms the situation in which a coalition of matchmakers opposes a coalition of rebels into one of triangles with hidden conflicting interests.[12] Even

---

Rosenblatt further specifies: "A family rule may be defined as a spoken or unspoken prescription that operates within the family to guide action" (129).

[11] Concern about family resemblance falls under the entity metaphor with its pathological dominance of an exaggerated need to express unity. In this context, the baroness expresses her "hopes and fears" (241) concerning the unity of her family, when she "came upon [...] a miniature of her brother, and sighed with a smile at the resemblance to his son. Hilarie surprised her at this moment, took possession of the portrait, and she, too, was strangely moved by the resemblance" (241) but not knowing yet how to define "strangely." Later on, as soon as Flavio appears dressed in his father's clothes "since his own clothes were unusable" (241) at the time, the baroness "smiled" (241) obviously welcoming the resemblance again, whereas Hilarie finds the image "uncanny, even oppressive" (241).

[12] In a "'family coalition,' two or more family members join together to achieve a goal or to oppose someone else in the family. [...] The metaphor of coalition

though coalitions and triangles create disharmony, the arising structural movement within the family weakens the power of the entity concept, and therefore provides an opportunity for redefinition and healing of each member and the family as a whole.

Before Hilarie's communicative breakthrough with her mother, closed communication patterns, however, function as a system control mechanism to continuously project the family as entity.[13] Rosenblatt defines the effects of open versus closed communication as follows:

> Family communication can be characterized on a dimension of openness to closedness. Relatively open communication involves a great deal of freedom to communicate thoughts, feelings, opinions, fantasies, and so on among family members. Openness also involves the freedom to communicate congruently, completely, and honestly. Relatively closed communication involves blocking, walling off, distorting, or denying thoughts, feelings, opinions, fantasies, and truths. The closing may involve choices about what to communicate and what not to communicate, as well as 'silencing strategies' (Zuk, 1965) to force compliance or conformity or to block or distort … communications. (158)[14]

Delaying and withholding information at times paired with ambiguity stand out as the dominant patterns of communication in the novella's family.[15] Closed communication thus mirrors the closed family system. For example, the baroness introduces her announcement to her brother that Hilarie is in love with him with the delaying remark: "You must first think a bit and guess" (213) Hilarie's choice. As the plot progresses, her letters completely conceal from her brother "that Hilarie's affection was undergoing a change" (246), unmindful of the amount of grief her brother would thereby suffer from finding out by surprise, because in a closed system "people are always closed about topics that at the moment are too

---

highlights heterogeneity in family relations and the ways in which family members do not function as individuals in relation to one another" (Rosenblatt 119). "Triangulation […] refers to a three-person relationship in which one person is adversely affected by the relationship of the other two. The term 'triangulation' is perhaps most often used when somebody is caught in the competition or conflict of two other people. The person caught in competing pressures is presumably distressed and has little room to maneuver" (Rosenblatt 117).

[13] Karnick argues in that the entire novel of the *Journeyman Years* essentially revolves around the problem of communication.

[14] See Zuk, 32-49.

[15] I am focusing here on verbal communication only; non-verbal communication through gestures and objects will be explored as part of a future project.

threatening for them to deal with and [...] that make the others anxious." (Rosenblatt 158) In the same fashion, the major also hides his true thoughts and feelings from his son, when he passes off his anticipated marriage to Hilarie as self-sacrifice to give Flavio "a way out" by saying: "old as I am, I would **have to** [my emphasis] marry Hilarie" (224) while "only with difficulty did the major conceal the joy that wanted to light up his face." (223) Communication changes from a closed to an open mode, when Hilarie tells her mother with conviction that she will not agree to the pre-arranged marriage with Flavio because of her broken commitment to her uncle: "Hilarie stood up, and before the judicious woman [her mother] could begin what she had to say, she began to speak." (249) Commencing with this assertive gesture, Hilarie stands her ground against her mother's persuasiveness and in the end wins her mother's respect as "the mother retreated, astounded at the nobility and dignity of the young girl, who energetically and truthfully articulated the unseemliness, nay, the infamy of such a union" (250). Even though Hilarie's moral position seems authentically hers, it might still originate in the fear of being morally judged by other women of her family as a "coquette" like the beautiful widow. Especially, Makarie, Hilarie's aunt and moral conscience of the family, "has held up a magic mirror of morality to some unhappy person" (252) including the beautiful widow. Moreover, the narrator criticizes Hilarie's change of affection retrospectively, when he reintroduces Hilarie as Flavio's wife into the main part of the novel mocking her "excessive ease in moving from one [love] interest to another of which we found her guilty in the course of our narrative" (401). Nonetheless, Hilarie gains the self-confidence that enables her to differ from her mother and to stand up for herself. Thus, Hilarie's temporary seclusion in her room that precedes the above confrontation becomes the first step in untangling her enmeshment with her mother, while the announcement of her renunciation and her departure from the estate for Italy become the second and third steps, respectively.

In conclusion, we learn from letters framing the novella's ending that Hilarie and the beautiful widow both leave their homes to set up their own residence in Italy for a while and after their return unite with the matches of their choice, Hilarie with Flavio, the beautiful widow with the uncle. Detached from her family of origin and strengthened in her own sense of identity by female companionship from outside of the family, Hilarie, released from family pressures, gains clarity over her own feelings and emotions.[16] As a result of this process of self-discovery, Hilarie chooses Flavio as her spouse based on her free will. Furthermore, despite outward appearance, their union does not result in the fulfillment of the parental marriage plan but creates new meaning by setting a new family goal that exceeds the family's previous vision of itself because the young couple joins a larger family-like community of expatriates to settle the New World, America, in order to pursue the founding of an utopian society based on their shared notion of social reform in which work replaces the value of landownership.

Works Cited

Bahr, Ehrhard. *Die Ironie im Spätwerk Goethes. '...diese sehr ernsten Scherze ...' Studien zum West-östlichen Divan, zu den Wanderjahren und zu Faust II.* Berlin: Erich Schmidt Verlag: 1972.

Bennett, Benjamin. *Beyond Theory: Eighteenth-Century German Literature and the Poetics of Irony.* Ithaca, New York & London: Cornell UP, 1993.

Elsaghe, Y. A. "'Helle' und 'Hölle:' Zur Rolle der Dichtung in *Wilhelm Meisters Wanderjahren*," *Goethe Yearbook* 7 (1994): 118-32.

Goethe, Johann Wolfgang von. *Conversations of German Refugees*, trans. Jan van Heurck in cooperation with Jane K. Brown, and *Wilhelm Meister's Journeyman Years or The Renunciants*, trans. Krishna Winston and ed. Jane K. Brown, *Goethe: The Collected Works*, vol. 10. Princeton: Princeton UP, 1994.

Hart, Gail. *Tragedy in Paradise: Family and Gender Politics in German Bourgeois Tragedy 1750-1850.* Columbia: Camden House, 1996.

Herweg, Henriette. *Das ewig Männliche ziehet uns hinab: Wilhelm Meisters Wanderjahre. Geschlechterdifferenz, sozialer Wandel, historische Anthropologie* (Tübingen & Basel: Francke, 1997).

Karnick, Manfred. *Wilhelm Meisters Wanderjahre oder die Kunst des Mittelbaren: Studien zum Problem der Verständigung in Goethes Altersepoche.* München: Fink, 1968.

Luhmann, Niklas. *Love as Passion: The Codification of Intimacy*, trans. Jeremy Gaines and Doris L. Jones. Stanford: Stanford University Press, 1998.

---

[16] Rosenblatt defines the bond formed between Hilarie and the beautiful widow as "sisterhood" and explains that "the sisterhood metaphor emphasizes how much women's relationships to other women are a source of strength, knowledge, support, healing, and groundedness" (117).

Mink, JoAnna Stephens and Janet Doubler Ward, eds. *The Significance of Sibling Relationships in Literature*. Bowling Green: Bowling Green State University Popular Press, 1993.

Muenzer, Clark. *Figures of Identity: Goethe's Novels and the Enigmatic Self.* University Park & London: Pennsylvania State UP, 1984.

Ponzi, Mauro. "Zur Entstehung des Goetheschen Motivs der 'Entsagung,'" *Zeitschrift für Germanistik* 2 (1986): 150-59.

Rosenblatt, Paul C. *Metaphors of Family Systems Theory: Toward New Constructions*. New York & London: The Guilford Press, 1994.

Salisbury, Isolde. *Goethes poetische Geschwisterpaare: Ihre Entwicklung, Funktion und Symbolik von den frühen Dramen bis zu Wilhelm Meisters Lehrjahren*, Europäische Hochschulschriften, Reihe 1, Deutsche Sprache und Literatur, vol. 1340. Frankfurt: Peter Lang, 1993.

Zuk, G. H. "On the Pathology of Silencing Strategies," *Family Process* 4 (1965): 32-49.

Chapter Six

Wordsworth's Mother Tongue: Mourning, Language, and Identity in "The Emigrant Mother"

Robert C. Hale, Monmouth College

> Too rigid a dichotomy of male subject and female object allows us to forget that, even according to men's depiction of themselves, subjectivity is initially produced through interaction with a woman. The Romantic tradition did not simply objectify women. It also subjected them, in a dual sense, portraying woman as subject in order to appropriate the feminine for male subjectivity.
> —Alan Richardson, "Romanticism and the Colonization of the Feminine"

In *Bearing the Word: Language and Female Experience in Nineteenth-Century Women's Writing*, Margaret Homans argues persuasively that romantic poetry "states most compellingly the traditional myth, as transmitted through literature, of women's place in language as the silent or vanished object of male representation and quest."[1] Other critics have also accepted masculine poets' tendency to objectify women in romantic literature. In her introduction to the very important collection, *Romanticism and Feminism*, Ann Mellor says, "The six male poets have been heralded because they endorsed a concept of the self as a power that gains control over and gives significance to nature, a nature troped in their writings as female. They thus legitimized the continued repression of women."[2] Marlon Ross argues that the female companion "allows the poet an external object (as an aspect of her otherness) to move toward in order to make real (to realize) his internal need (because she is also seen as an

---

[1] Homans, *Bearing the Word*, 40.
[2] Mellor, *Romanticism and Feminism*, 8.

aspect of the self)."³ Obvious examples such as the blessed babe section of book 2 of Wordsworth's *The Prelude*, Keats's "La Belle Dames Sans Merci," and Shelley's *Alastor* are just a few poems that can support these claims.

Critics often view William Wordsworth as particularly culpable in displaying insensitivity to gender issues and in objectifying women. For example, Ross argues that "Unlike Byron or Shelley, he never questions how the romantic poetic identity sustains sexual and political hierarchies."⁴ However, in several of his poems Wordsworth does represent women who have compelling voices. In particular, he represents mothers who are *present* subjects with powers of figuration and not simply silent or absent objects of quest.

Nonetheless, when critics examine mothers in Wordsworth's poetry, they typically explore the child/poet's relationship to an absent or dead mother who is often displaced onto a personified Nature. However, Wordsworth often represents active and present mothers who, conversely, *mourn* absent or lost children. Some of the more widely read mothers are unsuccessful in their mourning; for example, Margaret in "The Ruined Cottage" struggles to overcome the loss of her husband and children, and in "The Thorn" Martha Ray presumably laments the loss of an infant whom she may or may not have murdered. Conversely, in "The Emigrant Mother"—a lesser-known work from *Poems, in Two Volumes* (1807)—Wordsworth depicts a mother who has more success in mourning, uses poetic language to overcome her grief, and stabilizes her identity.

Traumatic events in Wordsworth's own life surely influenced this attention to mourning mothers. From a traditional psychoanalytic perspective, his interest might have been a manifestation of an unconscious desire to resurrect his dead mother Ann Wordsworth who died when he was almost eight. The poems then become an imaginative reversal of the child-mother positions, with mothers suffering the loss of children instead of a child suffering the loss of his mother, as the young Wordsworth certainly did. We might also interpret the interest as tied to guilt over his separation from his French mistress Annette Vallon and their daughter Caroline in 1793 because of the war with France. Within this framework, he perhaps displaces himself onto the child's position and becomes the absent one Annette desires, illogically punishes Annette for the pain the separation causes him by denying her the comfort of the child, and/or accurately depicts Annette's separation from Caroline since the

---

³ Ross, *Contours of Masculine Desire*, 93.
⁴ Ross, "Romantic Quest and Conquest," 49.

mother was initially not allowed to have her illegitimate daughter at home.[5] While all of these psycho-biographical readings are intriguing, I am more interested in reading the poems in terms of relational psychology and re-thinking some of the conventional wisdom about Wordsworth's representations of women and their relationship to his own poetics.

In the rest of the essay, I will first explain several connections between language, mourning, and poetic composition. Then, I will show how the emigrant mother uses (or is constructed as using) the same methods to mourn her son and construct a voice that Wordsworth uses to create poetry. While there are three mourning mothers depicted in *Poems, in Two Volumes* (Wordsworth also includes "The Sailor's Mother" and "The Affliction of Margaret" in the collection), the emigrant mother is represented with impressive powers of figuration and Wordsworth associates her mourning with her poetic faculties. He explicitly appropriates a woman's voice to write this poem; however, he renders her with the powers necessary to tell her storey, to form her identity, and to bring continuity to her life. This rendering moves us to a more complex understanding of Wordsworth's attitudes about gender, a view beyond the man-as-subject / woman-as-object scheme.

* * *

Coping with feelings of separation and connection is crucial to the developing child and to the mature adult: negotiating these two positions leads to children's development of language, serves as the springboard for childhood imaginative play which is the foundation of adult artistic production, and becomes the context for and means of adult mourning. Before I detail Wordsworth's association of these three activities and their relationship to the creative and receptive imagination, I will explain their similarities in the context of relational psychoanalytic theory. This context will help us to see the emigrant mother as a complex subject with whom Wordsworth, or at least his constructed narrator, identifies

According to Jacques Lacan's model of language acquisition, children begin to use symbolic language because of the perceived separation from the mother, and this separation, experienced as a sort of death, structures later substitution and figuration.[6] From Lacan's perspective, the infant

---

[5] Johnston, *The Hidden Wordsworth*, 317.

[6] My discussion of Lacan is based on his *Écrits: A Selection* especially "The Mirror Stage," 1-7, and "The Signification of the Phallus," 281-91; Julia Kristeva's *Desire in Language*, especially "From One Identity to Another," 124-

initially experiences no feeling of difference from the mother (the Imaginary state) and communicates in a sort of literal language of rhythm and tone (Kristeva's semiotic) which is unmediated—no difference is perceived between words/sounds (signifiers) and concepts (signifieds). However, the father, who possesses the phallus, intervenes in this potentially incestuous relationship; as a result, the phallus becomes the sign of difference from the mother, and of the difference between signifieds and signifiers. Lacan argues that with this awareness of difference from the mother, the child represses his desire for her, and consequently begins to replace the mother (the prohibited object) with symbolic language.

While Lacan's model illustrates the importance of separation and connection, it stresses separation from the mother at the expense of connection and does not recognize the importance of the mother's subjectivity, an issue central to poems about mourning mothers. Building on the work of Melanie Klein and D. W. Winnicott (among others), Daniel Stern views infants' development of identity and language as grounded in their growing awareness of similarity and difference with mothers as subjects. He argues that children have an *emergent sense of self and other* from birth and do not "experience a period of total self-other undifferentiation" as in Lacan's Imaginary stage.[7] Their awareness of difference and similarity culminates in what he calls a *verbal sense of self and other* in which children feel a loss because experiences of non-verbal attunement, experiences of "being with" the mother as in mutual gazes or nursing, must now be mediated by language: "Language forces a space between interpersonal experience as lived [experientially] and as represented" linguistically.[8] Paradoxically, language also enables infants to unite with their mothers "in a common symbol system, a forging of shared meaning. With each word, children solidify their mental commonality with the parent and later with the other members of the language culture."[9] Children receive the external stimuli just as they did before language, but also transform those stimuli into the new medium of language.

47; Eagleton's discussion of "Psychoanalysis" in *Literary Theory: An Introduction*, 131-68; and Margaret Homans's introduction to *Bearing the Word*, 1-39. See also Homans's account of a girl's different acquisition of language in *Bearing the Word*, 11-12.
[7] Stern, *The Interpersonal World of the Infant*, 10.
[8] Ibid., 182.
[9] Ibid., 172.

Winnicott's concept of the *transitional object* helps explain the connection between language acquisition and artistic power.[10] A transitional object is an object such as a blanket or stuffed animal that children use to master the anxiety of separation from their mothers. These objects occupy a "transitional realm" an "intermediate area of experiencing in which inner reality and external life both contribute."[11] Winnicott says this transitional realm between the infant and mother is a dimension that is neither internal nor external; it is an area of play in which the child "manipulates external phenomena in the service of the dream [the imagined object he sees] and invests chosen external phenomena with dream meaning and feeling."[12] According to Stern, early language also functions as a transitional phenomenon:

> the word is in a way 'discovered' or 'created' by the infant, in that the thought or knowledge is already in mind, ready to be linked up with the word. The word is given to the infant from the outside, by mother, but there exists a thought for it to be given to. . . . [the word] occupies a midway position between the infant's subjectivity and the mother's objectivity.[13]

As Susan Deri maintains, "Play, artistic creativity and appreciation are the direct natural successors to the early good transitional objects."[14] This kind of play with transitional objects, both toys and language, is the foundation for later adult artistic production—infants learn that they can reflect the impression of reality and distort that impression.

Balancing experiences of separation and connection is also important for successful mourning. Building mostly on the work of Sigmund Freud and Erik Erikson, Robert J. Lifton says that mourning is a survivor's

> struggle to reconstitute his psychic life in a way that can enable him to separate from the dead person while retaining a sense of connection with him, free himself from the deadness of that person and reestablish within himself, sometimes in altered form, whatever modes of immortality have been threatened by the death.[15]

---

[10] My description of transitional objects is greatly indebted to Schapiro's *Literature and the Relational Self*, 20-22.
[11] Winnicott, *Playing and Reality*, 2.
[12] Ibid., 51.
[13] Stern, *The Interpersonal World of the Infant*, 172.
[14] Deri, "Transitional Phenomena," 54.
[15] Lifton, *The Broken Connection*, 96.

He stresses the significance of both separation and connection, of accepting the loss of the other but paradoxically maintaining a connection with that person. The means to maintaining connection with the absent other is *symbolization*. For Lifton, symbolization is "the specifically human need to construct all experience as the only means of perceiving, knowing, and feeling."[16] Through symbolization in mourning the survivor re-orders the experiences of the other with enough difference to accept the real separation and with enough similarity to create continuity in the survivor's life. Lifton argues that "psychic numbing" or stasis overwhelms a survivor who cannot build this continuity; likewise, a survivor who creates too much connection becomes too dependent on (obsessed with) the absent other and cannot bring continuity to life. Infants mourn the loss of "direct contact with their own personal experience" because language never quite articulates lived experience; however, language becomes a compensation for the loss because it enables people to share lived experience with another person.[17]

Wordsworth himself associates language acquisition, poetic power, and mourning in the context of the mother-infant dyad in the "blessed babe" scene in book 2 of *The Prelude*. Barbara Schapiro considers this "eulogy" an ideal example of "the imagination as a form of transitional phenomenon arising out of the child's negotiation of separateness and union with the mother."[18] Wordsworth says,

>   blest the babe
> Nursed in his mother's arms, the babe who sleeps
> Upon his mother's breast, who, when his soul
> Claims manifest kindred with an earthly soul,
> Doth gather passion from his mother's eye.
> Such feelings pass into his torpid life
> Like an awakening breeze, and hence his mind,
> Even in the first trial of his powers,
> Is prompt and watchful, eager to combine
> In one appearance all the elements
> And parts of the same object, else detached
> And loth to coalesce.[19]

---

[16] Ibid., 6.
[17] Stern, *The Interpersonal World of the Infant*, 182.
[18] Schapiro, *Literature and the Relational Self*, 34
[19] Wordsworth, *The Prelude*, 1805 edition, 2.237-50. References to *The Prelude* are hereafter cited in text by line number.

For Wordsworth, feelings of identification ("manifest kindred") with the mother lead the child to imaginatively combine parts of the mother more fully into a unified other. He then describes the infant mind which is the model for the poetic spirit as "creator and receiver both" (274) and states that this experience is the "first / Poetic spirit of our human life" (275-76). These "mute dialogues with [his] mother's heart" (283) lead to a communion with nature, typically personified as maternal, and illustrate the receptive and creative imagination. The *receptive imagination* perceives and records stimuli and the *creative imagination* organizes and transforms them (Wordsworth's characterization of these faculties closely parallels Coleridge's description of the primary and secondary imagination in *Biographia Literaria*.[20] In the next part of book 2 "a trouble" comes into the babe's mind (291) because he becomes aware of the loss of the original relationship. Margaret Homans says this trouble is a feeling of loss "which feels like the mother's death, and it is, paradoxically, both caused by and the cause of representational language."[21] However, as Stern would explain, the child mourns the loss of the "direct contact" unmediated by language (the mother is still there), but gains the ability to share his lived experience (as the adult Wordsworth does in the act of writing *The Prelude*).

Wordsworth's discussion of his adult poetic process in "The Preface to *Lyrical Ballads*" helps clarify the relationship between mourning and poetic composition. He famously argues that poetry is

---

[20] Even though he does not use the terms *receptive* and *creative imagination* in the "Preface to *Lyrical Ballads*," he alludes to them and explains the importance of these poetic powers. In terms of the receptive imagination, he says that he wishes to keep his readers "in the company of flesh and blood," that he has "endeavoured to look steadily at [his] subject," and that he hopes his poems have "little falsehood of description" (45). In describing the poet's creative imagination, he says that he has endeavored to use "a certain colouring of imagination, whereby ordinary things should be presented to the mind in an unusual way," 40. Additionally, in the "Preface to the Edition of 1815" he uses the terms *Observation* and *Description*—"the ability to observe with accuracy things as they are in themselves, and with fidelity to describe them unmodified by any passion or feeling existing in the mind of the describer"—to refer to the receptive powers, and the terms *Imagination* and *Fancy*—"to modify, to create, and to associate"— to refer to the creative powers, 26. In *Wordsworth's Theory of Poetry*, James A. W. Heffernan writes lucidly about the receptive and creative powers though he refers to *reception* as *description* and *creation* as *Imagination*, see especially 6-29.
[21] Homans, *Bearing the Word*, 4.

the spontaneous overflow of powerful feelings; it takes its origin from emotions recollected in tranquillity: the emotion is contemplated till by a species of reaction the tranquillity gradually disappears, and an emotion, kindred to that which was before the subject of contemplation, is gradually produced, and does itself actually exist in the mind.[22]

His formulation of the beginnings of poetry has two basic parts: 1) an original experience from which he has been separated by time—the actual experience is "dead"; and 2) his recollection, his re-ordering or re-collection, of that experience. The recollection is not the same as the original but is "kindred" to it, similar to and yet different from it. Mourning a lost loved one follows a similar pattern. For Lifton, death separates the survivor from the absent other; then eventually, the survivor, in successful cases, reconstructs the other not only with enough difference to accept that person's actual death but also with enough similarity to establish a connection with him or her in order to affirm the continuity of life.[23] Mourning and poetic creation (as Wordsworth defines it) are structured similarly because both require separation from the original experience/other and also symbolic reconnection with the original that paradoxically accepts separation.

So far I have emphasized theoretical models conceptualizing mothers as subjects with whom children interact in order to show the relationship between language acquisition, mourning, and poetic power. Now, I would like to turn briefly to a discussion of why I think Wordsworth identifies with the emigrant mother. In his answer to the question "What is a Poet?" in "The Preface" (added in 1802, the same year that "The Emigrant Mother" was composed and the year he met Caroline), Wordsworth describes how a poet relates to his subjects: the poet brings

> his feelings near to those of the persons whose feelings he described, nay, for short spaces of time perhaps, to let himself slip into an entire delusion, and even confound[s] and identif[ies] his own feelings with theirs; modifying only the language which is thus suggested to him, by a consideration that he describes for a particular purpose, that of giving pleasure. (49)

---

[22] Wordsworth, "Preface to *Lyrical Ballads*," 57-8. I rely on Paul M. Zall's edition of "The Preface" (1802) because this version was published around the time "The Emigrant Mother" was composed. References to "The Preface" are hereafter cited in text by page number.

[23] Lifton, *The Broken Connection*, 96.

His process, thus seems similar to psychoanalytic theorist Jessica Benjamin's concept of *recognition*:

> that response from the other which makes meaningful the feelings, intentions, and actions of the self. It allows the self to realize its agency and authorship in a tangible way. But such recognition can only come from an other whom we, in turn, recognize as a person in his or her own right."[24]

Wordsworth sometimes stages a similar process when he displays the narrator's adoption of the mothers' voices. With the emigrant mother in particular he emphasizes the "confound[ing]" of his feelings with those of the mother, but at the same time, he separates himself with the use of language. He thus produces one of the most complex female voices in his canon.

* * *

In "The Emigrant Mother" Wordsworth presents a mother who has been separated from her son and tries to substitute another child for him.[25] As with "The Sailor's Mother" and many other poems representing the mother-child relationship (i.e., "The Norman Boy" and "The Force of Prayer"), Wordsworth begins this poem very self-consciously with a speaker who meta-poetically discloses the source of the poem or "lay."[26] In the introductory section, the narrator explains that he is friendly with a French emigrant, presumably in England because of the revolutionary wars. The narrator says that she has been separated from her own child, that she has often shared her "griefs" with him, and that the poem that follows is a song about what she "might say" to a neighbor child (12). At the end of the introduction he self-consciously says, "My song the workings of her heart expressed" to stress his identification with her (14).

---

[24] Benjamin, *The Bonds of Love*, 12.
[25] I should note explicitly from the beginning that the actual status of the mother's son is not certain—he may or may not be dead (the mother clearly hopes that he is not). Whether dead or alive, he is in France, and she cannot learn of his status for sure because the Napoleonic wars prevent her from returning crossing the Channel (in much the same way that Wordsworth was prevented from seeing Caroline). Whether he is dead or alive, the mother mourns the very poignant loss of contact with her beloved son.
[26] Wordsworth, *Poems, In Two Volumes*, p. 247, line 10. References to "The Emigrant Mother" are hereafter cited in text by line number.

The song is a combination of the narrator's understanding of the emigrant mother's experience and the narrator's own imagination; it is based on what the narrator "knew, had heard, and guess'd" (12-13). With this self-conscious, meta-poetic introduction, the poem becomes an example of Wordsworth's definition of poetry as the "spontaneous overflow of powerful feelings . . . recollected in tranquillity" and an enactment of his characterization of the infant mind which is the model for the poetic spirit as "creator and receiver both." The narrator "guesses" parts of the emigrant's storey, which is an overtly creative act because he is speculating. To tell what he "knows" or has "heard" from her is a receptive act because he describes what has actually happened. In the song section which follows the introduction, Wordsworth therefore represents the mother as relying on creative and receptive facets of her imagination to tell her storey and to mourn her son. By framing the song so explicitly with this narrator, Wordsworth emphasizes his practise of poetic identification, of the poet's "slip[ing] into an entire delusion, and even confound[ing] and identify[ing] his own feelings with" those he describes ("Preface," 49).

In the first stanza, the constructed mother describes the "'Dear Babe['s]'" separation from her real mother who is working in the fields (15). The emigrant mother suggests that the child could comfort her if she would be her child for "'one little hour'" (24). She then explains her separation from her son who apparently still lives in France, emphasizing the distance as "'A long, long way of land and sea'" (27). Next, she admits the possibility of complete separation from her son because he may be dead. Before leaving France the mother's tears fell on his face, and a nurse told her that such an act was "'"unlucky"'"; however, the mother then hyperbolically denies the act's unluckiness with a series of four *no*'s. After vehemently denying that her tears killed her son, she says that he will die because, according to those who take care of the child in the mother's absence, "'"He pines"'" (47). Here we have the narrator representing the mother as doing exactly what he has done with his introduction: she bases some of the storey on direct experience but then guesses in order to fill in the details about her child that she does not actually know, details that suggest a fantasy of identification. The mother hopes her son pines for her in the same way she obviously pines for him. Just like the narrator in the introduction, she bases the storey both on information that she has received and that she creates; her experience of loss leads her to develop a voice to construct a sense of reality (at least the narrator represents her as doing so). Consequently, Wordsworth represents strong identification between the narrator/poet and the mother in this poem.

However, the woman's creative and receptive imaginations come into conflict in the fourth stanza of her song. Her creative imagination fails to satisfy her when the narrator figures her as realizing that the little girl's "'chearful smiles'" and "'looks'" are not the same as her son's (49, 51). Despite her efforts to make the girl into her child, by stanza five, the illusion "'Tis gone—forgotten'" (55). She sees the smiles of her son in her mind's eye but recognizes that the smiles of the girl do not correspond (much as the mother of "Her Eyes Are Wild" who has difficulty when her son's actions do not meet her expectations). The little girl "'troublest'" and "'confound[s]'" her to the degree that she "'must lay [her] down'" (59-63). The receptive power of her imagination (knowing) overcomes her creative impulse (guessing). The mother consciously works through a fantasy and arrives at the reality of her situation as it is.

Her troubled state continues in stanza six as she attempts to substitute the present child for the absent one. The narrator constructs her as no longer trying to make the child into her son and explains that she loves the little girl for her own sake. She loves her even more than her sister's child who also lives nearby and "'who bears [the emigrant's] name'" (67). The French woman even goes so far as to say that "'Never was any Child more dear,'" which suggests that she loves the infant girl more than any other child, even her own son (74). She tries to erase the son to whom she can only connect through memory and to replace him with an actual, corporeal child who is present but not her own.

In stanza seven, however, this replacement strategy also fails. The verse paragraph begins with a very intrusive dash which marks an abrupt shift in the narrator's depiction of her thinking. The mother reveals that she "'cannot help it'" but that she must weep (75); she cannot replace her son. She fears that her tears and words do the girl-child harm, but then suddenly, the infant gives her a warm kiss which puts her heart "'again in its place'" (84). In a synaesthetic moment she says the child's eyes would "'speak'" to help her "'if they could'" (81-82). She receives the sensory impression that the child's eyes are on her, but she creatively embellishes the stimuli as the child's act of sympathy. Is the mother projecting her desire to be comforted onto the child, or could she be accurately interpreting the infant's intuitive attempt to console her? The final stanza suggests the latter.

The mother takes the original sense impression and reconstructs it with her creative imagination to give it a meaning. The narrator presents the emigrant mother as perceiving that the girl is not her son, but as finding "'contentment, hope, and Mother's glee'" in being with her (87). Even though she strongly identifies the little girl with her son by calling her "'by [her] Darling's name'" and saying her "'features seem to [her] the same,'" the emigrant mother says, "'His little Sister thou shalt be'" (90-93). Thus, the mother achieves a balance between the receptive and creative facets of her imagination. She receives the sense impressions that indicate the girl is not her son and recognizes that the girl is not her own, but she also and at the same time recognizes that the child is enough like her son that she can make her into a close substitute. Just as with Jessica Benjamin's description of the mother who feels recognized by her newborn, the emigrant mother not only projects her feelings onto the girl, but also acknowledges that the girl is different from her son:

> To experience recognition in the fullest most joyful way, entails the paradox that 'you' who are 'mine' are also different, new, outside of me. It thus includes the sense of loss that you are [. . .] no longer simply my fantasy of you.[27]

Because of Wordsworth's detailed depiction of *recognition*, this mother is one of the most fully delineated subjects that he creates. She connects/identifies with another subject, but she does not merge her identity with his (as does the mother of "Her Eyes are Wild"). She does not become, in Lifton's terms, "static."[28] She is aware of and accepts her ability to fantasize and uses that power to mourn her loss. She achieves the same balance that the narrator describes in the opening prologue. More than any other mother Wordsworth creates, she is overtly self-conscious.

But what about the narrator's depiction of the mother's response to her son? As her experience with the present girl is decidedly one of recognition, her experience with her absent son (or her mental image of him) is one of successful mourning. The mother struggles to put order back into her life after being separated from her country and child by "free[ing] [her]self from the deadness" or absence "of that person" and "retaining a sense of connection with him."[29] She attempts to create a figure of her son in the girl (to make the girl into her son), but discovers that strategy is ineffective. She then decides to replace him completely with the girl and also finds that approach futile. Finally, she accepts her

---

[27] Benjamin, *The Bonds of Love*, 15.
[28] Lifton, *The Broken Connection*, 6.
[29] Ibid., 96.

separation from the son and her uncertainty about his absence or death and also accepts that the girl is not her child, but very consciously *plays* as if she is.

Wordsworth's depiction of this play further augments the sophistication of this female subject. Susan Rubin Suleiman argues that playing is

> the activity through which the human subject most freely and inventively constitutes herself or himself. To play is to affirm an "I," an autonomous subjectivity that exercises control over a world of possibilities; at the same time, and contrarily, it is in playing that the I can experience itself in its most fluid and boundaryless state. . . . To imagine the mother playing is to recognize her most fully as a creative subject—autonomous and free, yet (or for that reason?) able to take the risk of 'infinite expansion' that goes with creativity.[30]

Just as the girl will "play" with "grass" and "flowers," the emigrant will play with the child: she "'will call [her] by her Darling's name'" (89-90). Her mourning play, in effect, allows her to tell the storey of her separation from her son. She is not completely bound by the restrictions of reality and uses the creative and receptive components of her imagination (Wordsworth represents her as doing this) to adjust to the loss of her son. The fact that when she returns to France, she will "'tell [her son] many tales of'" the girl not only makes her differentiation between son and surrogate daughter clear, but it also suggests that the emigrant's strategy for mourning the loss of the little girl when she returns to France will be narrative: she will tell her son about "'His little Sister'" (93).

The special complexity of this poem is that Wordsworth overtly represents the poem as the narrator's rendering of the emigrant mother's mourning: "My song the workings of her heart expressed" (14). Like the mother he figures, Wordsworth plays too. In a sense he appropriates a woman's voice to write his own poem, but he gives his female representation the creative and receptive powers that he possesses—the ability to recollect and reconstruct "her" storey and construct a complex moment of recognition. He also represents the mother as being able to represent other characters who tell stories—the mother tells of the nurse who told her: "'"Tears should not / Be shed upon an Infant's face / It was unlucky"'" (41-43). Because he represents the mother as telling her storey, incorporates the words of others into her storey, and achieves a balance of

---

[30] Suleiman, "Playing and Motherhood," 280.

separation and connection, she is not just a vanished object of quest. Just as with Wordsworth's representation of himself in *The Prelude*, and all subjects represented in poetry, she is an object of Wordsworth's representation, yet she, unlike some poetic objects, is also portrayed with a complex voice to tell her storey. In this poem, Wordsworth depicts mourning and poetic composition in process.

* * *

Mourning and figuration are both highly evolved acts of agency because they involve testing and balancing inner and outer worlds. In "The Emigrant Mother," Wordsworth plays with the paradoxical dynamic of separation and connection that is the foundation of figuration, that is crucial to mourning in order to bring continuity to life, and that is so important to his own theory and practise of poetry. Wordsworth's reversal of the typical pattern of child-seeking-absent-mother with mother-seeking-absent-child makes "The Emigrant Mother" especially striking. By reading poems with mothers who mourn as central characters, and there are at least ten in his canon, we can begin to see that Wordsworth does not always simply objectify women. In fact, he also conceptualizes them as figures who experience, suffer, endure, and order losses—the very actions that critics such as Geoffrey Hartman have taught us to see as central to canonical works such as *The Prelude* and "Tintern Abbey" and to Wordsworth's work in general but which have been presented primarily from a child's (Wordsworth's) perspective. In effect, these poems can show that Wordsworth did not always simply separate or distinguish himself from mothers, but that indeed he identified with them, especially in a poem such as "The Emigrant Mother" where he meta-poetically stages the identification, not as a narcissistic merger, but explicitly as play, testing the boundaries between self and other.

Critics rarely, if ever, read "The Emigrant Mother," or other poems depicting present, mourning mothers such as "The Sailor's Mother," "The Affliction of Margaret," "The Force of Prayer," "The Norman Boy," or "Maternal Grief" to name just a few. I think one reason may be because they follow the conventional wisdom about Wordsworth as, in Judith Page's words, "appropriator of women and the feminine for an exclusively male poetic enterprise which ultimately denies women their subjectivity."[31] I agree with Page that the conventional wisdom is often over-simplified. Wordsworth's play with the motif of mourning mothers

---

[31] Page, *Wordsworth and the Cultivation of Women*, 2.

reveals a poet who is uncertain about how to cope with separation. He certainly experiences feelings of separation himself, but he also observes and imagines it in others. Language and the imagination become the means of coping with the separation, language and imagination that arise out of feelings of separation and longings for connection.

Works Cited

Benjamin, Jessica. *The Bonds of Love: Psychoanalysis, Feminism, and the Problem of Domination*. New York: Pantheon, 1988.
Deri, Susan. "Transitional Phenomena: Vicissitudes of Symbolization and Creativity." In *Between Fantasy and Reality: Transitional Objects and Phenomena*, edited by Simon A. Grolnick and Leonard Barkin, 45-60. New York: Jason Aronson, 1978.
Eagleton, Terry. *Literary Theory: An Introduction*. 2nd ed. Minneapolis: University of Minnesota Press, 1996.
Homans, Margaret. *Bearing the Word: Language and Female Experience in Nineteenth-Century Women's Writing*. Chicago: University of Chicago Press, 1986.
Johnston, Kenneth. *The Hidden Wordsworth: Poet, Lover, Rebel, Spy*. New York: Norton, 1998.
Kristeva, Julia. *Desire in Language: A Semiotic Approach to Literature and Art*. Translated by Thomas Gora, Alice Jardine, and Leon S. Roudiez. New York: Columbia University Press, 1980.
Lacan, Jacques. *Écrits: A Selection*. Translated by Alan Sheridan. New York: Norton, 1977.
Lifton, Robert Jay. *The Broken Connection: On Death and the Continuity of Life*. New York: Simon and Schuster, 1979.
Mellor, Anne K., ed. *Romanticism & Feminism*. Bloomington: Indiana University Press, 1988.
—. *Romanticism & Gender*. New York: Routledge, 1993.
Page, Judith W. *Wordsworth and the Cultivation of Women*. Berkeley: University of California Press, 1994.
Pollock, George H. Vol. 2. Of *The Mourning Liberation Process*. Madison, WI: International University Press, 1989.
Richardson, Alan. "Romanticism and the Colonization of the Feminine." In Mellor, *Romanticism and Feminism*, 13-25.
Ross, Marlon B. *The Contours of Masculine Desire: Romanticism and the Rise of Women's Poetry*. New York: Oxford University Press, 1989.

—. "Romantic Quest and Conquest: Troping Masculine Power in the Crisis of Poetic Identity." In Mellor, *Romanticism and Feminism*, 26-51.

Schapiro, Barbara A. *Literature and the Relational Self*. New York: New York University Press, 1994.

Stern, Daniel N. *The Interpersonal World of the Infant: A View from Psychoanalysis and Developmental Psychology*. New York: Basic Books, 1985.

Suleiman, Susan Rubin. "Playing and Motherhood; or, How to Get the Most Out of the Avant-Garde." In Bassin, *Representations of Motherhood*, edited by Donna Bassin, Margaret Honey, and Meryle Mahrer Kaplan, 272-82. New Haven: Yale University Press, 1994.

Winnicott, D. W. *Playing and Reality*. 1953. New York: Basic Books, 1971.

Wordsworth, William. "The Preface to *Lyrical Ballads*." In *Literary Criticism Of William Wordsworth*, edited by Paul M. Zall, 38-62. Lincoln: University of Nebraska Press, 1966.

—. "Preface to the Edition of 1815." Vol. 3 of *The Prose Works of William Wordsworth*, edited by W.J.B. Owen and Jane Worthington Smyser, 15-52. New York: Oxford University Press, 1974.

—. *The Prelude: 1799, 1805, 1850*, edited by Jonathan Wordsworth, M. H. Abrams, and Stephen Gill. New York: Norton, 1979.

—. *Poems in Two Volumes, and Other Poems, 1800-1807*, edited by Jared Curtis. The Cornell Wordsworth. Ithaca: Cornell University Press, 1983.

CHAPTER SEVEN

REFORMING THE SPACE OF THE CHILD: INFANCY AND THE RECEPTION OF WORDSWORTH'S "ODE"

DAVID B. RUDERMAN, UNIVERSITY OF MICHIGAN

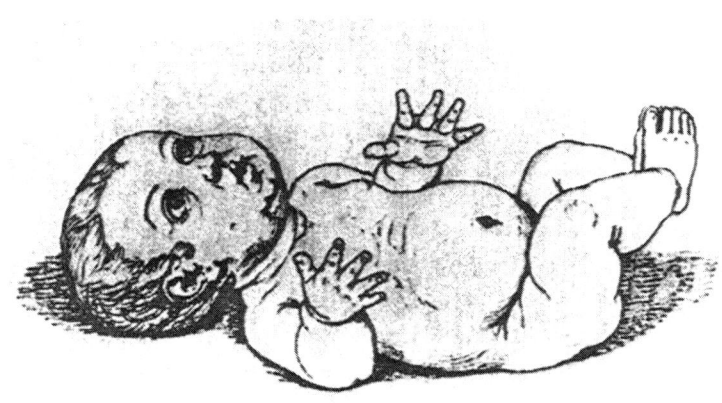

Historically, in Wordsworth studies as well as in poetry criticism more generally, the use of psychoanalysis has largely resulted in a criticism that seeks to "explain" features of the poetry in light of the poet's personal losses (e.g., Wordsworth's early loss of both parents), repression, parapraxis, etc.[1] The best of the newer work focuses on melancholy in its many modern and post-modern permutations.[2] These studies tend to

---

[1] See for example Plotz and Wilson.
[2] See Battan and Wilner.

centre, for obvious reasons, on *The Prelude*. My approach here is different in at least two, perhaps related, ways: I focus on a work—"The Intimations Ode"—that is not about the "growth of a poet's mind" (i.e., does not attempt to describe or recapitulate a process of "development"), and I am not primarily concerned with trauma or (political or personal) loss.

Instead, in this essay I employ selected psychoanalytic terms and concepts in order to build a reception history of Wordsworth's Ode so as to situate within a contemporary context the poem's (in)famous apostrophe to the six years darling, as well the theory of immortality (and its anterior existence) implied by that figure. Both have become tropes for such concepts as poetic origination, unmediated sensory experience, and access to a numinous realm. Drawing on more recent work from British object relations theory as well as the contemporary philosophic theories of Giorgio Agamben and Julia Kristeva, I show how Wordsworth's "spatialization of infancy" (revealed, in part, through its particular historical reception) puts pressure on the received notions of *bildung* that continue to organize our readings of romantic poetry and poetics. Specifically, I show how the idea or experience of the child functions in the period, not as temporal stage, to be preserved/overcome (i.e., sublated) in the process of development, but rather as a "position" readily accessible to the adult subject. The payoff of this revisionary model is that it gives us a picture of subject formation driven neither by a process of identification and normalization (as in J. S. Mill's account of the Ode) nor by skeptical repudiation (as in Matthew Arnold's). This critical construct (teased out of Wordsworth's poetry and prose) offers a third way. Embracing a model of experience that is "split" (incorporating intuition *and* reason), fluid rather than fixed, horizontal rather than vertically arranged, spatiality suggests an ethics and politics (of the child and thereby the self) that is neither stagist nor productivist. The conflation of the space of the child with the aesthetic space of the poet further complicates and deepens this picture. It opens up new possibilities for conceiving of the aesthetic dimension as only one of several "positions" available to the subject. Thus at the heart of Wordsworth's poetry and poetics, often evaluated as quietist and regressive, we find the kernel of a radical difference, the deterritorialized space of the poetic child.[3]

---

[3] My concept of spatiality finds resonances with Timothy Morton's concept of an ambient poetics. For Morton, an ecological, ambient being-present is suggested by several of Wordsworth's poems, something he terms a "depthless ecology." Similarly, I'm interested in an anti-depth model of subjectivity, suggested by the

My reading does not attempt a phenomenology of the child, is not, in fact, about the child at all, but rather about the *relation* between representations of the child and the adult poet/reader/viewer. As such, "natural piety," as revealed through the poetic space of infancy, does not reinscribe a sense of purity within the represented child. Instead, it marks the absence of the *need* for such concepts/judgments (purity, corruption, etc.) altogether.[4] The central metaphor for this in my essay is Freud's influential yet brief description of ego "splitting" in "Splitting of the Ego in the Defensive Process." The child chooses not to choose between pleasure and reality, or chooses to have them both (Freud says this amounts to the same thing).[5] Choosing not to choose is to be two places, two persons at once. Because, in this split model, there is no *telos* or loss, it defies organic processes of unification and signals a relaxation of the drives. "Becoming" (in other words, the production and reproduction of a self) is undone by the lack of necessity for choosing, while the ethos of nostalgic "return" is subverted because, as the logic of the Ode itself has it, we can "*in a moment* travel thither."

Lodged in this essay's account of these revisionary processes is a question about what it means that our sense of who and what we are in the world is still wedded to models of depth and narratives of development. I believe we can hear echoes of "absolute spirit" in recent American political rhetoric that characterizes the most recent war in Iraq as "a struggle between freedom and tyranny" and a "path to lasting security," a struggle in which there is "no middle ground."[6] No middle ground and no child left behind – these narratives of certainty, duty, progress, and paternalism lean heavily on models of liberalism and development, of "recapitulation," of internal and external struggle (nationalism arising in an incestuous and reciprocal relation to individualism [think of Coleridge's "political writing" in *The Friend*])[7], all of which we can see

---

spatiality of the child in the Ode and present in Wordsworth's theory of immortality.

[4] I am using Wordsworth's term "natural piety" in the sense that Anne-Lise Francois (re)defines it, as a "kind of trust and openness to contingency" (63).

[5] Freud defines the concept of defensively splitting the ego as: "a conflict between the demand of the instinct and the prohibition by reality. But in fact the child takes neither course, or rather he takes both simultaneously, which comes to the same thing. He replies to the conflict with two contrary reactions, both of which are valid and effective" (275).

[6] Washington Post online: http://www.washingtonpost.com/wpdyn/content/article/2006/03/13/AR2006031300813.html

[7] Coleridge writes in issue 1 that all of his ideas are "not suggested to me by Books, but forced on me by reflection on my own Being, and Observation of the

reproduced if not concretized in many of our narratives of infancy. One premise of this essay is that an intensive reading of the reception of Wordsworth's Ode reveals an ethics or politics of infancy in which a depthless relation to the child and to the remembered self slowly begins to take shape.[8] And it is against the backdrop, and through the cracks of Arnold's conservative skepticism of the child (his fear of singularity and otherness) and Mill's wholesale incorporation of its figurations (his faith in the power of a universal narrative) that the lineaments of this spatiality can be glimpsed.

Wordsworth's "Bad" Philosophy and The Role of the Child

It may seem odd to begin an exegesis of the poetry of romantic childhood and experience with Matthew Arnold, an author who is skeptical of, if not entirely opposed to, the value and availability of these terms.[9] But it is precisely this ambivalence that makes Arnold's reading of Wordsworth so productive. In fact, Arnold's 1879 edition of Wordsworth's poems is a kind of reformation or rephrasing in its own right, in that it attempts a wholesale cleansing or classicizing of Wordsworth's poetic legacy.[10] In its preface, Arnold refers to the "Intimations Ode" as the cornerstone of Wordsworth's "bad philosophy."

Ways of those about me, especially of little Children" (8). What follows of course (his system) consists of Coleridge's political, religious, and aesthetic views, the tenor of which has been commented on thoroughly, usually under the critical rubric of his "romantic ideology."

[8] See Henderson for a revision of the conventional critical view that theories of the subject in the romantic period were exclusively tied to models of depth (1-10). Regarding the importance of memory to models of depth, Beth Lau usefully revises the work of memory in Wordsworth's poetry away from the "Freudian model" towards recent developments in cognitive and neuroscience (676). Yet while Lau writes that these discoveries "challenge many of Freud's notions," the claims she makes for memories ("determined by our interests," "colored" by our moods) are strikingly similar to Freud's own claims in "Screen Memories," and would seem to validate his theories rather than refute them (677).

[9] Reading Wordsworth through his historical reception by Matthew Arnold allows us to see how the infant/child *evolves,* how it *functions* as a trope in the poetry of the period at the same time as it *presents itself* as a topos. C.f. William Empson in his essay on *Alice in Wonderland* in which he argues that the Victorian image of the child-as-judge suggests a model of subjectivity more conflicted about "return" than earlier "romantic" versions; the figure of the swain is displaced, reflecting a culture more "open to neurosis" (254).

[10] See Curtis' discussion of Arnold's revisionary editing of Wordsworth (44 -57).

It is a philosophy, he insists, that must be dismissed in order that the poetry itself might be appreciated. Centreing on the "idea of the high instincts and affections coming out in childhood," it fails because it is not universally true. Not everyone, says Arnold, possesses an immediate connection to nature as a child; "many people, perhaps the majority of *educated* persons" have no connection to nature at all as children, but rather find the love of nature "strong and operative" later in life (my emphasis).[11] Arnold's refusal of Wordsworth's ontology of the child shows us (a) that he is a good historicist critic, seeking to historicize the particular conditions of childhood, the child, and love of nature by refusing their predicative idealization; (b) that the liberal "turn to nature," popularized though not inaugurated by the Lake poets, had already made its way so far inside of culture as to have effaced its point of entry; and (c) that by denying the child its transcendental origin, we are left with a vacant, vulnerable, and pre-subjective child, one that is prefigured elsewhere in Wordsworth's poetry (chiefly, in the *Lyrical Ballads),*[12] and one that in various formes will continue to haunt Arnold and all of Anglo-American poetry down to the present.[13] The (useful) threat that Arnold's reading poses for mainstream theories of romanticism and phenomenology is that by denying the *particularity* of the remembered child and/or childhood, we risk impoverishing experience by refusing its power to guarantee a sense of self, reducing it to static *singularity* or to mere contingent incident.

Of course, the discourse of the particular and the universal is one of the central concerns of Romanticism generally, and of Arnold's aesthetic theory more specifically.[14] There is, in fact, an uncanny similarity, if not

---

[11] Arnold's reading has ethical and epochal overtones in that it shifts the focus away from Wordsworth's interest—which following on Rousseau, Erasmus Darwin, etc., focuses on the child under the rubric of natural philosophy—towards the situation of the reader. Thus, perhaps responding to the historical tenor of the times, Wordsworth's ontological interest becomes, for Arnold, epistemological.

[12] See Marjorie Levinson's *Wordsworth's Great Period Poems* in which she suggests an important distinction between the child in the *Lyrical Ballads* and the Pindaric or odal child in the Ode (96, 97).

[13] At the risk of schematizing, I suggest that two related strains of poetic representations of childhood follow after Wordsworth, one that sets up child/childhood/memory as a place of possibility for rebirth or creative work (i.e. overcoming or compensating loss), and one in which child/childhood/memory stands merely as the location and remainder of that loss. In terms of 20th century American poetry, Bishop and Duncan fall into the former category, whereas Eliot and Berryman fall into the latter.

[14] See Kelley for the problem of the "particular" in 19th-century poetry.

homology, of terms and concepts in Arnold's statements about the Wordsworthian child on the one hand, and his statements about poetry and aesthetics in general on the other. This relation itself can be contextualized within the canon of romantic poetry, which tends to reproduce the child (its body, its sounds, its futurity) as the space of poetic or aesthetic encounter; the sleeping infant or playing child metonymically comes to stand for the aesthetic object or poem itself.[15] It is here that we can recognize the power of Arnold's intervention. He initially recognizes a split or inconsistency in Wordsworth's philosophy in the Ode: his particular cannot be universalized. This split, which Hegel claims can be answered only through transcendence to Absolute spirit, is never sublated in Arnold's critique of Wordsworth. It is either (depending on your point of view) elided or endured, as it is in his larger critical project as well. Although Arnold severs philosophy from poetry in the *Function of Criticism at the Present Time*, there is no place for the particular, the contingent, for difference, in either realm.[16] Philosophy must be the place of universal truth, and poetry must evoke universal themes. It must be disinterested. It must teach us how to live.[17]

Besides repudiating Romantic notions of childhood and the child, Arnold's banishment of stubborn and anomalous particularity deals a double blow to received concepts of romantic poetic creation. It refuses the trend toward unification as it effaces the Hegelian absolute subject, who, being incarnated like Christ, is the perfect marriage of universal and particular. In fact, given the close metaphoric equation of childhood, nature, and poetic voice and vocation in book one of *The Prelude*, one could even say that, in terms of Wordsworth's poetics, by banishing the child from a de-sublimated nature, it banishes the possibility of lyric

---

[15] Think of Blake's "Infant Joy," Baille's "A Mother to her Waking Infant," Byron's address to Ada book-ending Canto III of *Childe Harold's Pilgrimage,* Coleridge's "Frost and Midnight" and "Nightingale: an Ode," or Wordsworth's own "Blessed be the Babe" passage from *The Prelude.*
[16] *The Function of Criticism in the Present Time* (237).
[17] For Hegel the reconciliation of particular and universal is exemplified in the person of Christ, whom the artist must emulate (77).
For Arnold, it is not enough (ala Coleridge's edict) to exemplify the universal. A third feature is necessary, history: "...for the creation of a master-work of literature two powers must concur, the power of the man and the power of the moment..." ("Function of Criticism" 238). Criticism's job is to bring the moment/idea/epoch to fruition; the poet's job is to express it. See also the preface to Wordsworth's collection pg. 343.

expression altogether.[18] Thus, Arnold's critique allows us to see that it is *precisely this gap between the particular and the universal, between experience and recognition, between intuition and concept, which childhood generally represents, and which romantic childhood and, by extension, poetic vocation, is miraculously meant to transcend.* The strain that this places on the poetic child is evinced in the hyperbolic descriptions of the child in the "Ode," which drew such objections from Coleridge in the *Biographia Literaria*.[19] It further accounts for the double-bind set up in late-eighteenth and nineteenth-century natural history, philosophy, and moral psychology, which require that the child be entirely "for itself" (even in its intense vulnerability), even as these discourses seek relentlessly to observe, regularize, and categorize the child.[20] The incommensurability of these aims – these splits that seem not merely inherent in the child and to our discourse, but somehow constitutive of it – is what each poetic articulation attempts to "forme over," to make appear as one organic unity.[21]

---

[18] "Was it for this / That one, the fairest of all rivers, loved / To blend his murmurs with my nurse's song....sent a voice / That flowed along my dreams?" (*Prelude* 1805, lns. 269 – 274). By banishing Wordsworth's myth of poetic origin, Arnold has dismantled both the poem's narrative structure (its interrelated movement from strophe to antistrophe to epode), as well as its affective urgency, its apostrophic interruptions of temporality. For apostrophe, see Jonathan Culler, 148. For the identification of voice with nature in Wordsworth, see Jacobus.

[19] Coleridge reads Wordsworth critically, but in a different direction than Arnold (see below). He insists that that the "best philosopher" should correspond to received or current conceptualizations of philosophy: " In what sense is a child of that age a *philosopher*? In what sense does he *read* 'the eternal deep'...by reflection? by knowledge? by conscious intuition? or by *any* forme of modification of consciousness?" (7, II: 138).

[20] Rousseau epitomizes the incommensurability philosophy imposes between particular and universal in Emile: "Natural man is entirely for himself...civil man is only a fractional unity dependent on the denominator...good social institutions are those that best know how to denature man, to take his absolute existence from him in order to give him a relative one and transport the "I" into the common unity..." (39,40). For an overview of the uses of the child in the 18th-century sciences see Benzaquén.

[21] See Jerome McGann (4-10). For a dissenting view of organicism see Charles Armstrong.

"Have known too much—or else forgotten all"

Arnold's own poetic encounters with the child are marked by a similar malformation or split, as his anxious catechizing of the voiceless, enigmatic child in these opening stanzas of his earlier poem "To a Gipsy child by the Seashore" makes clear.[22]

> WHO taught this pleading to unpractised eyes?
> Who hid such import in an infant's gloom?
> Who lent thee, child, this meditative guise?
> Who mass'd, round that slight brow, these clouds of doom?
>
> Lo! sails that gleam a moment and are gone;
> The swinging waters, and the cluster'd pier.
> Not idly Earth and Ocean labour on,
> Nor idly do these sea-birds hover near.
>
> But thou, whom superfluity of joy
> Wafts not from thine own thoughts, nor longings vain,
> Nor weariness, the full-fed soul's annoy—
> Remaining in thy hunger and thy pain;
>
> Thou, drugging pain by patience; half averse
> From thine own mother's breast, that knows not thee;
> With eyes which sought thine eyes thou didst converse,
> And that soul-searching vision fell on me.

In what might be read as a return of the repressed, the disenchanted Gipsy child with its "pleading" and "unpracticed eyes," is refused voice and generalization in nature. In fact, despite the preposition in the title of the poem – "Child *by* the Seashore"[23] – the child seems entirely denied spatiality[24]; its only context is its non-context as a figure of alterity within

---

[22] Perhaps there is a way to understand Arnold's refusal of his own "Empedocles on Etna" on the grounds that it did not offer answers as an attempt to banish the child or the ambivalent from his own work – see Isobel Armstrong's *Victorian Poetry* (208 –214).

[23] Isobel Armstrong comments on Arnold's "estranging sea" (228).

[24] The scene itself is anthropomorphized, seen as labouring and in constant motion. Nothing grounds the child, not even its mother who "knows not thee" (14). Arnold did try in a failed revision to orient the reader and mute the hyperbolic power of the first stanza's questions: "The port lies bright under the August sun, / Gay shine the waters and the cluster'd pier; / Blithely this morn, old Ocean's work is done, And blithely do these sea-birds hover near" Allott (23).

a larger frame of otherworldliness. Arnold's question "WHO taught this pleading to unpracticed eyes" responds to and reframes Wordsworth's earlier question "WHERE is it now, the glory and the dream?" Unlike the "Ode," the poem cannot adduce an origin for the child. It does not speak; and neither does the poet directly interpose.[25] The poem does however attempt several implied identifications. Arnold, in a series of similes rather than apostrophes – refigurations rather than concretizations – compares the child to a hermit, an exile, an angel, and finally to a stoic.[26] The formal use of simile (the child is *compared* to something rather that named: "thou best philosopher") revises the organic unity of the Ode. It is though the child (in the poet's imaginative need to *figure* it) is in costume, or better, in drag. Identity is kept separate and distinct: child = stoic = poet = poem = self (although one could easily rearrange or reverse the order). The ultimate reversability reflected by line 48: the child having "known too much – or else forgotten all" performs beautifully this uncanny slippage. It is strangely arrested, undecided, marked by a medial caesura and a dash.[27] (Later in my essay, I will argue for a connection between Arnold's poetic undecidabilty and what I call Wordsworth's spatialization of infancy. Each suggests a revision of developmental models of subjectivity in favour of a poetics of relation or "position.")

Arnold's placeless child in "Gipsy Child by the Seashore" is a logical antecedent of a nature that no longer requires poetic interpretation, and a logical descendent, or perhaps distant relative, of the evacuated child that Arnold's critique of the Ode infers. It haunts (the poet and us) not only because it has no place in nature but also because it has no history, no

---

[25] If, as I have suggested, the child operates tropologically in the poems of the period, then the poem and child are, if not identical, then so closely and reciprocally connected as to suggest an umbilical relation. Notice for example the tendency for time and narrative to be arrested whenever the child is given actual voice in the poem (i.e. is represented as speaking or is quoted); the poem itself seems threatened with collapse. Some examples of this phenomenon are: "Infant Joy," "Anecdote for Fathers," and "We are Seven."

[26] Throughout Arnold's poetic corpus, the stoic philosopher as well as the liminal figure of the gipsy occupy a privileged place (e.g. "Thyrsis" and "The Scholar Gipsy").

[27] Whereas Arnold could argue for a more historically accurate accounting of the child in Wordsworth's Ode, his historicizing project breaks down when it comes to his own poetry and the child: i.e., his inability to recognize or represent the (social, economic, political) conditions that might have produced the pleading eyes of the Gipsy child.

memory proper to it.[28] Hunger and pain ("Remaining in thy hunger and thy pain") while very nearly idealized as precursors to "vision," are refused historical determination. Denied a verifiable inside, the exteriority of the child (and thus the poet) is complete. The other (nature, mother, reader, child) remains fixed and external. Although the unrecognizability of the child reproduces a discomfort with difference and encroaching cultural and ethnic otherness and foreignness that Arnold expresses elsewhere in his criticism (and which Wordsworth equally expresses, most notably in this case, in his poem the "Gipsies"), here, in Arnold's poetry, the anxiety cannot be theorized or even fully owned.[29] Instead we get projections and repeated vain attempts to analogize the child.[30] Psychically, the poet needs to situate the child (temporally, spatially, historically, and culturally) in order to establish and secure his own relation to it. Yet as mightily as he struggles, the child remains opaque. Thus, the circle of gloom (poet to child and back again) cannot be squared by acts of associated imaginative selections from Arnold's own personal past; nor can it find a frame of reference within the indexical codes of nationality (the exile), religion (the angel), or poetic or philosophic legacy (the stoic). The text that I'm alluding to (and expanding on) here is, of course, Freud's "Screen Memories," a text which explains the mechanisms by which memory and imagination are able to reconstruct history and thereby manage pain, confusion, and disappointment in the present.

Arnold's poetic/philosophic/aesthetic refusal of the particular is instructive, as is his anticipatory ambivalence about Freud's retrospective romanticization (itself, a reversal of Wordsworth's transcendental deduction in the Ode: "having been, must always be" becomes, in Freud, "being now [remembered], it must have happened, or else have been merely wished"). As we will see from Mill's therapeutic experience of reading the Ode, bad philosophy can be both contagious and curative. For Mill, subjectivity is a project, but one that in his adaptive "affective" method, can never be entirely free from the knowledge that it owes its origin to someone or something other.

---

[28] Giorgio Agamben makes explicit the connection between children and ghosts. Both operate within society as unstable, yet necessary signifiers; without them, "there would be neither human time nor history" (84).

[29] For Arnold's extreme discomfort with encroaching otherness, see *Culture and Anarchy* (527-557).

[30] Compare the idleness of the gipsies in Wordsworth's "Gipsies" to Arnold's claim that "Not idly Earth and Ocean labour on, / Nor idly do these sea-birds hover near" (7, 8).

The Metaphysics of Memory

> What made Wordsworth's poems a medicine for my state of mind, was that they expressed, not mere outward beauty, but states of feeling, and of thought coloured by feeling, under the excitement of beauty. They seemed to be the very culture of the feelings, which I was in quest of.[31]

J. S. Mill's autobiographical narrative of overcoming a depression (the result, he claims, of an "unnatural" and "experimental" education) by reading Wordsworth's poetry is one of the most well-known and fascinating accounts of the salutary, even life-saving, effects of poetry. Mill begins by establishing a triad of poets for consideration. Byron, whom Mill knows and acknowledges is the superior poet, cannot relieve Mill of his dejection. Coleridge proves perfect for describing his dilemma but is unable to affect a cure. Mill ultimately discovers Wordsworth, whose poems, and more to the point, *philosophy*, seem tailor-made for Mill's recuperation. It is with the Ode, and specifically its evocation of the child, that Mill ultimately identifies. Yet his identification is neither with the child nor with nature exactly, but rather with the poet himself: "I found that he too had had similar experience to mine; that he had felt that the first freshness of youthful enjoyment of life was not lasting; but that he had sought for compensation, and found it, in the way in which he was now teaching me to find it" (105). Mill's reading is allegorical, even analogical in the extreme. But in order to see how the figure of the child is still functioning, even defensively *driving* Mill's account, we need to remember that what first began to "cure" the philosopher of his dejection was not Wordsworth or poetry at all. Rather, Mill had be "reading, accidentally, Marmontel's memoirs," when he:

> came to the passage which [Marmontel] relates his father's death…and the sudden inspiration by which he, then a mere boy, felt and made them feel that he would be everything to them—would supply the place of all that they had lost. (99)

From this moment, writes Mill, his "burthen grew lighter" (99). It does not, or should not, surprise us that Mill, who was in many ways haunted or shadowed by his father's life, should now be moved or "lightened" by the storey of the death of the father. Furthermore, the "mere boy" in the

---

[31] From the *Autobiography of John Stuart Mill* (104). As I describe below, I take Mill's account of already conditioned beauty as deriving its value precisely from its mediatory function.

narrative can be read as kin to the imagined child in the "Ode"—the child as father of the man. Thus, the prose narrative opens up an imagination of the father's death—an ego death to the degree that the internalized father is cast out—that makes room for, or precipitates another, more affective object to enter. That object, I am arguing, is only partially the child in the "Ode," but even more properly the poet. The child serves as a synecdoche for the feeling voice of the poet within the redemptive narrative of the poem. And it is with this "recovered" child that the philosopher identifies.

But what is most strange about Mill's identification is his evocation of a "first freshness of youthful enjoyment." There does not seem to be any trace of these feelings in Mill's descriptions of his early life in the autobiography. As I have said, it is almost as if the poem and the figure of the child make possible a reclamation of what never was. Perhaps this is not surprising given that the "Intimations Ode" itself plays out its redemptive themes on the razor's edge of seeming and being: "There was a time when meadow, grove, and stream, / the earth, and every common sight, / To me did *seem* / Apparelled in celestial light" (1-4). This qualification of appearance—remember Wordsworth's injunction against the "tyranny of the eye"—begs the question as to whether this was truly a glorified state of awareness or the mere appearance of perfection, a nostalgic side effect of memory.[32] Later in the poem's penultimate stanza the poet grounds his invocation of the philosophic mind in the essentializing logic of "primal sympathy": "having been, [it] must always be" (183). Thus, employing a similar logic, Mill is able to construct an idealized childhood indirectly through his triangulated identification with the "best philosopher of the poem"—what in more conventional psychoanalytic terms we would call the incorporated child within the poet.[33]

---

[32] It may surprise some readers that I have thus far bracketed Wordsworth's own mention of Platonism in connection with this poem (Wordsworth *Fenwick* 61). I take the comment (spoken at a retrospect of several decades) as an attempt to absolve himself of accusations of apostasy, rather than as an accurate description of the poem or its philosophical contexts.

[33] As I hope is becoming clear, it is not Mill's identification, as such, that I find troubling as a model, but rather that he conditions all identifications on the predication of loss. This melancholic relation to infancy and the child seems to require the symbolic language of "depth." I will argue in what follows for another model, in which "position" or "transition" replaces incorporation (or introjection) as the central explanatory developmental conceit. For a theory of incorporation as a failed attempt at introjection see Abraham and Torok (125-138).

As the slippage from being to "seeming" suggests, there is an explicit tension in this passage between the conceptualization of the theoretical space of infancy as a place of putative (imaginative or literal) return and that of a displacement or "re-placement." In the latter configuration, the space of the child formes an *a priori* condition, necessary to the ideological or mythical function of the poem. In fact, most commentators read the ambivalence that Wordsworth expresses as precisely the cost of such compensation, effects of the strain the reality principle dictates.[34] Mill himself, in the course of defending Wordsworth in debate, understood the "mere animal delights" of an earlier time to be irrecuperable; they are *replaced* by others.[35] But this should not surprise us, for as we have seen, for Mill the culture of feeling must be established through an active (i.e. aesthetic) reconstruction of a *fictive* childhood.

Infancy and History

Whereas Mill's constructed "return" shows the dangers and benefits of projective identification, Arnold's poems show the dangers and benefits of imagining a child who is denied a transcendent origin.[36] In attempting to correct Wordsworth's ideological universalizing of idealized childhood, Arnold returns to and reinforces the myth of the child as poet and poet as child. The identification with the silent child that Arnold establishes in "Gipsy Child" through the constant evocations of "gloom" (his own as well as the child's), leads to the final stanza, which prophesizes an imminent return. But it is unable to call forth what Abrams terms the "ritual language of...blessing" ("Structure" 227). Immediacy and experience are simultaneously imputed to the child and refused. A "chain" of grief is what remains, to crown and link the just-anointed child to the poet. The return of the child that Arnold imagines in the final stanza is an inversion of Mill's Schillerian return, whereby the poet/philosopher goes back in imagination to childhood and returns with a "state of nature in idea, which is not indeed given him by experience," but is rather an

---

[34] Trilling, Bloom, etc.
[35] "He has painted all the successive states of his own mind. 1. the mere animal delights received from the beauties of nature. 2. the decay of those feelings, and their being replace by those others which have been described" (441).
[36] There is a sense in which, following Freud's famous formula, Arnold represents a melancholic relation to experience, whereas Mill demonstrates the more normative functioning of compensatory mourning. For a definition of projective identification (a process whereby one splits objects into "good" and "bad" and projects the bad object out onto others) see Klein (181-186).

"ultimate aim," provided by reason, and "borrowed" from this ideal state (28). Because in Arnold's poem there is no "state of nature" (in idea or elsewhere)—i.e., there is no space or place or memory to which one might return—the Gipsy-Child "comes up" instead from within (the culture, the poet), but also from without (i.e., the devastated mise en scene). It leaves the poet, and us, nowhere spatially or temporally to go. In other words, like so many of Wordsworth's *Lyrical Ballads*, Arnold's poem refuses dialectical closure, even as it refutes the hard-won flicker of experience in the Ode.

Philosopher Giorgio Agamben claims that this inability to access experience is one of, if not the primary, conditions of modernity. He further locates this (human) condition in, what he calls the "historico-transcendental dimension" of infancy. Infancy is the theoretical crux because it precedes discourse; it is the "transcendental origin of language."[37] Agamben does not idealize this state, as do Piaget or some readings of Lacan's "Ideal-I" stage.[38] There is no "pre-subjective 'psychic substance'" any more than there is a "pre-linguistic subject" (48). Language and experience coexist and are mutually constituted. The change or difference that infancy signals is the move from the semiotic (babble/nature/experience) to the semantic (discourse/culture/history). Rather than being described as a "fall," it is more of a transition. And, although inevitable, Agamben imagines this transition as reversible, open, and non-teleological. Following and building on Benveniste, he claims that the semiotic and the semantic are "the two transcendental limits which define and simultaneously are defined by man's infancy" (55).

As a way of establishing the points of convergence between Agamben and Wordsworth's theory of infancy and immortality, I want to return to the supposed scene of synthesis or closure in the Ode, the passage from stanza 9, crucial to so many 20th-century critical accounts of the Ode (Wimsatt, Bloom, Hartman, Fry):

---

[37] Infancy, according to Rousseau, was the first stage of the child's life and ended at 5 years old. Extending this state and focusing it on language development, Phillipe Aries, in *Centuries of Childhood,* suggests that the transition from infancy to the next stage (*pueritia*) is predicated not so much on language acquisition, as on verbal mastery (21).

[38] "This jublilant (sic) assumption of his specular image by the child at the *infans* stage, still sunk in his motor incapacity and nursling dependence, would seem to exhibit in an exemplary situation the symbolic matrix in which the *I* is precipitated in a primordial forme, before it is objectified in the dialectic of identification with the other, and before language restores to it, in the universal its function as subject. This forme would have to be called the Ideal-I…" (Ecrits 2).

> Hence in a season of calm weather
> Though inland far we be
> Our souls have sight of that immortal sea
> Which brought us hither,
> Can in a moment travel thither,
> And see the Children sport upon the shore,
> And hear the mighty waters rolling evermore.
> 165-171[39]

What is being offered I would argue is neither synthesis, return, nor epode, rather a spatialized point of origin. Experience (immortality) may be accessed (seen, heard) at any time, at any point. This crossing over is neither dialectical nor total. The ephemeral connotations of "soul" are partially undone by the sensuality of sight and hearing.[40] What our souls *see* are the children sporting; what we *hear* are the mighty waters—which for Wordsworth are translations of—or sounds available for translation into—poetic voice, but for Arnold (think of "Dover Beach" or "Gipsy Child") are simply self-estranging.[41]

As I have suggested, the temporal spatiality of "in a moment travel thither" suggests unhindered transport (back and forth) between the socialized world of the semantic and a semiotic, pre-Babel state. Part of Wordsworth's innovation is to *spatialize this split*—in several of the *Lyrical Ballads* (including "There was a boy…" and "The Thorn") and in the epode of the Ode ("Hence in a season of fair weather, though inland

---

[39] Bloom, in an early reading of the Ode, sees this passage as intensely vital. He is primarily focused on the disjunction between sight and sound, and never comments on what I see as the crucial problem of the passage, i.e., that it is our "souls" that are supposed to see and travel. He literalizes and externalizes the distance in the passage, while admitting the immortal (i.e. metaphysical) nature of the sea, as well as its "Arnoldian" confirmation of our "separateness" (*Visionary* 187, 188). Interestingly, in a later reading of the passage, he reads this same moment as a collapse back into solipsism, thus suggesting that the distance is internal or imagined (*MOM* 146, 147). Either way, he reads it as alienating. Trilling, in his famous demythologizing reading of the Ode avoids the passage altogether. He uses Ferenzci and Freud to speak of a kind of undifferentiated space of the child, and even follows Freud (via *Civilization and its Discontents*) back into the womb of the mother (*L I* 140).

[40] See "Tintern Abbey", in which much of the structure of this section (the separating out of the soul ["we are laid asleep / In body, and become a living soul:" (45, 46)], the kinds of soulful [i.e., mental/emotional/spiritual] seeing and hearing) is already foregrounded.

[41] For Arnold's concept of the "poetic soul" see his essay on Gray: "genuine poetry is conceived and composed in the soul" (*Essays* 149).

far we be..."). The spatialization of infancy arises as a response to the problem of particularization ("But there's a Tree, of many, one, / A single Field which I have looked upon, / Both of them speak of something that is gone"). William Wimsatt's well-known reading of the Ode obliquely implies that the Ode offers a model wherein infancy/experience can be imagined spatially, as a site that is not external;[42] the distance between the sea and inland, which can be traveled (by the soul—thus internally) in an instant, represents the collapsed immediacy of experience, the possibility of what Sartre calls a "universal singular."[43] Whereas Arnold's gipsy poem holds everything in abeyance, locked into a skidding universe of empty signification, the Ode's bad philosophy, its spatialized infancy allows for movement, mutuality, and modification, as indicated by the privileging of the murky, qualified, and vertiginous states of vanishings and blank misgivings – in other words, ambivalence.

Looking back then at the Ode, the move from semiotic infancy to the semantic dimension of meaning can be located in its most often criticized stanza 7.[44]

> Behold the Child among his new-born blisses,
> A six years' Darling of a pigmy size!
> See, where 'mid work of his own hand he lies,
> Fretted by sallies of his mother's kisses,
> With light upon him from his father's eyes!
> See, at his feet, some little plan or chart,
> Some fragment from his dream of human life,
> Shaped by himself with newly-learned art;
> A wedding or a festival,
> A mourning or a funeral;
> And this hath now his heart,

---

[42] Here is Wimsatt's description from *The Structure of Romantic Nature Imagery:* "The question for the analyst of structure is: Why are the children found on the seashore? In what way to they add to the solemnity or mystery of the sea? Or do they at all? The answer is that they are not strictly parts of the...vehicle, but the...tenor, attracted over, from tenor to vehicle. The travellers looking back in both space and time *see themselves as children on the shore*, as if just born like Venus from the foam" (Bloom 87 – my italics).

[43] Sartre: "For a man is never an individual; it would be more fitting to call him a *universal singular"* (50).

[44] Interestingly, twentieth-century critics (Wimsatt, Bloom, Hartman, Fry) all seem to focus on the epode. All seem unanimous that the ode does not resolve (Hartman calls pseudo-Pindarics "epiphanic abortions"), yet to my knowledge only Hartman (along w/ Coleridge) identifies stanzas 7 and 8 as the crux of the problem and the poem. (206).

And unto this he frames his song:
Then will he fit his tongue
To dialogues of business, love, or strife;[45]

The child is seen as always-already within the semiotic world of cultural, familial, and religious signs, but he "shapes" them *by himself* (92) Conceptually, this shaping corresponds to Kristeva's semiotic *ordering*, which precedes semantic conceptualization (27). Within the poem, we can track the progression of participles and verbs from the materiality of "shaping" to the ambiguous signification of "hath" (either his heart *has* or it is *had*, or both), and finally, to the less hard to follow "frames." I would argue that it is only when he strives to "*fit* his tongue / To dialogues of business, love, or strife" (93, 94) that he enters fully into the semantic dimension of discourse.[46] But again, this crossing of a limit does not constitute an entrance into a symbolic order from which the child cannot return. It does not consist of a movement from one stage to another as in Freud's oral, anal, and genital phases. Rather, it consists of *occupying a position*.[47] While the semantic is the world of others, of order, of negotiation and dialogues rather than self-created songs, or fragments of dreams, it is also the realm of the universal, of discourse, of reflection. In part, what I am suggesting is that one function of poetic infancy is to show us how it might be possible to mediate (or shuttle) between these states or positions. Agamben further suggests that to understand this crossing-over we must move beyond our received, enlightened understandings of origin: "The origin of a 'being' of this kind cannot be *historicized,* because it is itself *historicizing,* and itself founds the possibility of there being any 'history'" (49).[48] I take Agamben's philosophical gloss on infancy to be roughly consonant with many psychoanalytic understandings of the child, experience, and language (Kristeva and Green certainly, Lacan and Klein more partially).

---

[45] In the 1807 edition Wordsworth revised the child's age upward from 4 to 6, in order to have it correspond to Hartley Coleridge's age at the time of composition (H Hartman 143).
[46] Again, the shift is not from prelingual to lingual, but rather from language to "mastery." See note 38 above.
[47] "Klein's concept of the 'position,' then, invokes neither a 'stage'…nor a 'structure…[it describes] a shifting psychic vantage point" (Kristeva *M. K.* 66).
[48] Carolyn Steedman has written on the connection in the late-eighteenth/early-nineteenth centuries between the romantic child and the emerging idea of human interiority. Jacqueline Rose and James Kincaid have commented on the impossible bind this places on the discursive child, and through him, on us.

So far I have been arguing for a revisionist or reconstructed reading of the Ode, which takes into account its theorization of immortality, what I have called the space of the child. I have pointed out that the space of the child orients the child (vis-à-vis Kant's first critique) externally, whereas the temporality of the child is oriented always-already internally. Wordsworth's genius is to drive the two together through the figure of a *soul that sees*. Reading this figure through Freud, Klein, and Winnicott (et al) reveals the psychological implications of mutually contaminated subjects and objects, at the same time as it theorizes these processes (already present in the poetry) through concepts such as positionality, splitting, transitional phenomena, and transference. Arnold's reception of the Ode, and his own poetic incorporation of its content, suggest a deep Wordsworthian ambivalence, that strangely only resolves itself (i.e., gives us material to interpret) around the issues of poetic forme, or as he has it, the question of Wordsworth's style (which in some ways is identical to the question of origin). Mill's investment in, if not investigation of, the space of the child also offers itself as a study of the aesthetic space of the poem, or as he has it, in the privileging of feeling over eloquence (348).[49] As we will now see, Wordsworth's theory of immortality, sketched out in more detail in his prose, prefigures a structural account that allows for the non-exclusive co-existence of reason and intuition, feeling and eloquence, an intellectual intuition.

Wordsworth's "Intermediate Thought" of Immortality

Wordsworth opens his 1810 essay "Upon Epitaphs" with a disquisition on the necessity of feelings or intimations of immortality. These feelings, he suggests, are grounded in our infancy, and "the time is not in remembrance when, with respect to our own individual Being, the mind was without this assurance" (127). Wordsworth is at pains to explain the unique mechanism within us that would cause us to desire recognition even after our deaths. "Mere love" he writes, could not have produced it. It seems that this narcissistic desire exists in us at (or *as)* the very limits of the animal and the human. A dog or a horse, which perishes in the field, cannot anticipate the sense of sorrow that his death will cause for his fellow animals. Yet even our faculty of reason, when added to the principle of love "which exists in the inferior animals," is still not enough to account for the desire in humans (126). Some other force or principle is

---

[49] See Nancy Yousef for a description of Mill's efforts to prize the aesthetic or sensual from the moral or rational.

at work. There must be some "intermediate thought." Wordsworth names this the "intimation or assurance within us, that some part of our nature is imperishable" (127).

Wordsworth does not really explain why a sense of imperishability should necessarily lead to a desire for recognition after death (this would seem to be a secondary narcissism where one might expect precisely an easing of such tension).[50] He concentrates instead on its genesis, claiming that the desire for recognition does not develop until the "*social* feelings have been developed, and the Reason has connected itself with a wide range of objects" (127). "The sense of immortality," he continues, "if not a coexistent and twin birth of Reason, is among the earliest of her offspring: and we may further assert, that from these conjoined, and under their countenance, the human affections are gradually formed and opened out" (128). Thus, somewhat uncharacteristically for Wordsworth, he claims that, in this account, reason is the factor that precipitates feeling and affection.[51] But it is reason twinborn or pregnant with a sense of immortality. The schema looks something like this:

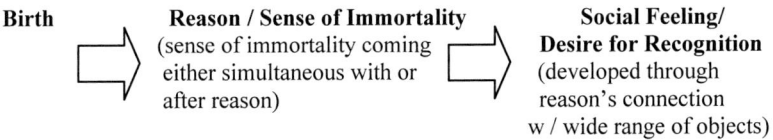

This diagramme shows that, consonant with a whole body of recent criticism, Wordsworth's model of creativity, spirituality, and development (i.e., that which is most prized) is something that occurs prior to and in the absence of any connection to the social or familial.[52] The child, like a flower, unfolds.[53]

---

[50] Fear of death enters Wordsworth's essay only in the negative – as a frost that would chill the spirit if the intimations of immortality were gone. Later, in describing the first requisite of epitaphs (that the language should sink into the heart), he locates "the two points in which all men feel themselves to be in absolute coincidence" – birth, and death (136).

[51] See Wordsworth's claim in the preface that he was placing sentiment prior to, but not subordinate to, rationality (62, 63).

[52] See, for example, Yousef.

[53] This depiction of "unfolding" departs in ways that are, as is characteristic of Wordsworth, both politically radical and potentially quietistic. In contrast, Schiller paints a picture in *The Aesthetic Education of Man* of the philosopher/poet as being always already politicized: "He comes to himself out of his sensuous

And yet, as a theory of infancy, Wordsworth's renovation drives a forme of reason into the sensual, without the need for Kantian concepts, as a Kleinian *position* rather than a Freudian stage.[54] Perhaps this is why, to Coleridge and others, the Ode is so profoundly moving *and* frustrating. Furthermore, by seeking to allow an intuitive forme of experience for the child, Wordsworth proleptically allies himself with Hegel and Benjamin.[55]

So much of the recent discourse on the child in the eighteenth and nineteenth centuries focuses on the child as a figure for what is internal to the self, as a kind of ur-figure of interiority.[56] Far from wanting to deny or distance myself from this view, I've tried to show how Wordsworth's conception of experience and immortality complicates this picture, not by giving it depth (I was tempted when typing just now to write "death"), but by strangely flattening it out, by spatializing it.

M. H. Abrams, in *Natural Supernaturalism* writes of Schiller's Universal History as attaining the shape of a spiral.[57] Wordsworth's theory

---

slumber, recognizes himself as Man, looks around and finds himself—in the State" (28).

[54] I have already brought forward the concept of position in the forme of Giorgio Agamben's philosophical positing of the semiotic as a transcendental limit. Kristeva also uses the concept of position to argue for a semiotic state, similar to Agamben's, something she calls, via Plato, the chora: a realm that is not organized according to a "law (a term we reserve for the symbolic) but through an *ordering*" (27). I'm interested in the possibility that, when taken together with some of the other features of Wordsworth's aesthetics, positionality might represent a component of a radical aesthetic, an aesthetics of infancy, a poetic and subjective concept that allows for a freer, unhindered and "nonregressive" movement, which Freudian "stages" simply do not allow or imply. A poetry and ethos of "position" would complicate our critical accounts of the *strictly* linguistic "fall" into the symbolic, perhaps displacing somewhat our suspicion of the aesthetic realm as constitutive or evident of yet another universal master code.

[55] For Hegel's desire to recapture an intellectual intuition in Kant, see Guyer; for a reading of Benjamin's desire to "extend Kant's concept of experience towards an intuitive forme of experience" see Linroos (22).

[56] "The modern concept of the self – which took shape throughout the nineteenth century and was formalized in early twentieth-century psychoanalysis – is grounded in a distinctive view of childhood as the depths of historicity within individuals. Childhood is entangled with the adult's present identity because the interiorized self, the sense of a self within, is perceived as internalized memory of the past, the outcome of a personal history." Benzaquen 36

[57] Taking the reader through an overview of the biblical-recaptitualist philosophies of Lessing, Kant, and Schiller, Abrams shows how a narrative develops whereby the individual, as well as the collective, move (through the processes of a fortunate fall) from innocence/instinct into reason. Once we move through the subsequent

of immortality, as we have seen, functions differently. In his model, a kind of reason is "twinborn" with instinct and immediate experience. As I indicate in my introduction, the change that I am trying to ring on the grand narrative of Romanticism has to do precisely with this flattening out. Rather than reading the Ode (as it has sometimes been read) as a return to formes of Christian Platonism, I am suggesting a more relaxed reading of infancy and childhood (via Wordsworth, Arnold, and Mill), one that is non-productivist and non-redemptive. At the same time, over and against conventional critical "depth" models of traumatic poetry, of "spots of time," I've been trying to tell the tale of a non-melancholic space of the child, one that does not "take in" or incorporate experience but simply experiences, in a more horizontal arrangement (somewhat like an infant who puts objects in her mouth to know the world; ninety-nine times out of one hundred, she won't swallow). Put another way, I have been trying to read *loss and recuperation not as objects but as spaces*—"immortality" as a "style" in the sense that Foucault suggests as being indexical of modernity in his essay "What is Enlightenment?"

Geoffrey Hartman, that most ethical and exacting of critics, ends the essay "Reading, Trauma, Pedagogy" by claiming that testimony goes hand in hand with trauma. The close relation of testimony to trauma, makes it seem as though, as a discourse, poetry itself is a traumatized genre, compelled to tell its storey out of some deep wound. And perhaps, to some extent, it is. But as deeply ethical as Hartman's vision is, I still want to resist it in favour of something else. I worry about this equivalence of poetry with post-traumatic stress syndrome, where the child or poem now becomes compelled to speak, as in some Foucaultian scenario of confession. This interrogation room of the child/poet is the polar opposite of the space of the child I'm attempting to paint. I've been trying to envision a poetry that tells things in its own time and way, a riddling child/poet, whose silence, strange, or enigmatic verse might sometimes makes us nervous—something like Arnold's Gipsy Child. D.W. Winnicott himself is attuned to the need for allowing the reader/patient to arrive at her own interpretations:

> It appalls me to think how much deep change I have prevented or delayed in patients…by my personal need to interpret. If only we can wait, the

historical and individual stages, we will be able to affect a return. But this return will not be circular, as in previous Platonic/Christian formes, but rather in a spiral, where the return is a return with a difference, i.e., at a higher level. Reasoned innocence or instinct thus comes (for the first time) into the world. But it only arrives through suffering and hard (aesthetic/philosophical) work (199-217).

patient arrives at understanding creatively and with immense joy, and I now enjoy this joy more than I used to enjoy the sense of having been clever. (86)

This to me seems an equally ethical way to proceed, and not one, I think, with which Hartman would disagree. So I want to conclude by acknowledging a parallel between Winnicott's patient deferral of interpretation (employing as it does, a sense of Wordsworthian "joy") and what Anne-Lise Francois has called Wordsworth's "ethos of receptivity toward the natural world" (59). It strikes me that this split description is precisely the space of the child I have been trying to adduce, the poem as an analytic space of transference and transition, a fractured and ambivalence space, where interpretations come quietly and of their own accord, a space that does not lie too deep for tears, but is always already there, and here.

Works Cited

Abraham, Nicolas and Torok, Maria. *The Shell and the Kernel: Renewals of Psychoanalysis, Vol. 1.* Chicago; London: The University of Chicago Press, 1994.

Abrams, M. H. "Structure and Style in the Greater Romantic Lyric" *Romanticism and Consciousness: Essays in Criticism.* Ed. Harold Bloom. New York: W.W. Norton, 1970.

—. *Natural Supernaturalism: Tradition and Revolution in Romantic Literature.* New York: W. W. Norton, 1971.

Agamben, Giorgio. *Infancy and History: The Destruction of Experience.* Trans. Liz Heron. London; New York: Verso, 1993.

Aries, Phillipp. *Centuries of Childhood.* trans. Baldick. London: J. Cape, 1962.

Armstrong, Isobel: *Victorian Poetry: Poetry, poetics, and politics.* New York: Routledge, 1993.

Arnold, Matthew. *Culture and Anarchy. The Portable Matthew Arnold.* Ed. Lionel Trilling. New York: Penguin, 1980.

—. "The Function of Criticism at the Present Time." *The Portable Matthew Arnold.* Ed. Lionel Trilling. New York: Penguin, 1980.

—. "Wordsworth" *Essays on English Literature.* Ed. F. W. Bateson. London: University of London Press, 1965.

—. *The Poems of Matthew Arnold.* Ed. Kenneth Allott. London: Longman's Greenand Co., 1965.

Batten, Guin. *The Orphaned Imagination : Melancholy and Commodity Culture in English Romanticism.* Durham : Duke University Press, 1998.

Benzaquén, Adriana. "Childhood, Identity and Human Science in the Enlightenment." *History Workshop Journal.* 57, 2004.

Bloom, Harold. *A Map of Misreading.* New York: Oxford University Press, 1975.

—. *The Visionary Company: A reading of English Romantic Poetry.* New York: Anchor/Doubleday, 1963.

Coleridge, Samuel Taylor. *The Collected Works of Samuel Taylor Coleridge.* Ed. James Engell, and W. Jackson Bate. 16 vols. New Jersey: Princeton University Press, 1983.

—. *Friend* from *The Collected Works of Samuel Taylor Coleridge.* Ed. Barbara Rooke. Bollingen Series. London; New Jersy: Routledge, 1969.

—. *The Portable Coleridge.* Ed. Richards. London; New York: Penguin, 1950, 1978.

Culler, Jonathan. *The Pursuit of Signs.* New York: Cornell University Press, 1983.

Curtis, Jared. "Matthew Arnold's Wordsworth: The Tinker Tinkered" *The Mind in Creation: Essays on English romantic Literature in honour of Ross G. Woodman.* Ed. J. Douglas Kneale. Quebec: McGill-Queens University Press, 1992.

Empson, William. *Some Versions of Pastoral.* New York: New Directsions, 1974.

Francois, Anne-Lise. "'O Happy Living Things': Frankenfoods and the Bounds of Wordsworthian Natural Piety" *Diacritics.* 33.2: 42-70.

Freud, Sigmund. "Screen Memories." *Collected Papers Vol. V.* Ed. James Strachey. London: Hogarth Press, 1953.

—. "Splitting of the Ego in the Defensive Process." *Collected Papers Vol. V.* Ed. James Strachey. London: Hogarth Press, 1953.

Fry, Paul. *The Poet's Calling in the English Ode.* New Haven: Yale University Press, 1980.

Guyer, Paul. "The Rejection of Kantian Dualism" *Cambridge Companion to German Idealism.* Ed. Karl Ameriks. New York: Cambridge, 2002.

Hartman, Geoffrey. *The Unremarkable Wordsworth: Theory and History of Literature, Volume 34.* Minneapolis, University of Minnesota Press, 1987.

—. "Reading, Trauma, Pedagogy." *The Geoffrey Hartman Reader.* Ed. Geoffrey Hartman & Daniel T. O'Hara. New York: Fordham University Press, 2004.

Hartman, Herbert. "The Intimations of Wordsworth's Ode." *The Review of English Studies* 6. 22 (1930): 129-48.
Hegel, Georg Wilheim Friedrich. *Introductory Lectures on Aesthetics.* Trans. Bernard Bosanquet. New York: Penguin, 1993.
Henderson, Andrea K. *Romantic Identities: Varieties of Subjectivity 1774-1830.* Cambridge; New York: Cambridge University Press, 1996.
Jacobus, Mary "Apostrophe and Lyric Voice in *The Prelude*" *Lyric Poetry: Beyond New Criticism.* Ed. Hosek and Parker. Ithaca; London: Cornell University Press, 1985.
Kelley, Theresa M. "Romantic Nature Bites Back: Adorno and Romantic Natural History. *European Romantic Review.* 15.2: 193-203.
Kincaid, James. *Child-loving: the erotic child and Victorian culture.* New York: Routledge, 1992.
Klein, Melanie. *The Selected Melanie Klein.* Ed. Juliet Mitchell. New York: The Free Press, 1987.
Kristeva, Julia. *Revolution in Poetic Language.* Trans. Margaret Walker. New York: Columbia University Press, 1984.
—. *Melanie Klein.* Trans Ross Guberman. New York: Columbia U P, 2001.
Lacan, Jacques. *Ecrits: A Selection.* Trans. Alan Sheridan. New York: W. W. Norton, 1977.
—. *.The Four Fundamental Concepts of Psychoanalysis.* Trans. Alan Sheridan. New York: W. W. Norton, 1981.
Lau, Beth. "Wordsworth and Current Memory Research" *Studies in English Literature 1500-1900.* 42.4: 675-692.
Levinson, Marjorie. *Wordsworth's Great Period Poems; Four Essays.* Cambridge, Eng: Cambridge University Press, 1986.
Lindroos, Kia. "Scattering Community: Benjamin on Experience, Narrative and History." *Philosphophy & Social Criticism.* 27:6 (19-41).
McGann, Jerome. *Romantic Ideology: A Critical Investigation.* Chicago, 1983.
Mill, John Stuart. *Autobiography of John Stuart Mill.* New York: Columbia University Press, 1944.
—. "Wordsworth and Byron." *Journals and Debating Speeches: The Collected Edition of the Works of John Stuart Mill.* Ed. John M. Robson. Toronto; Buffalo: University of Toronto Press, 1988.
Morton, Timothy. *"Why Ambient Poetics? Outline for a Depthless Ecology."* Wordsworth Circle. Winter 2002.
Plotz, Judith. *Romanticism and the Vocation of Childhood.* New York: Palgrave, 2001.

Rose, Jacqueline. *The Case of Peter Pan, or, The Impossibility of Children's Fiction.* London: Macmillan, 1984.

Rousseau, Jean Jacques. *Emile or On Education.* Trans Allan Bloom. New York: Basic Books Inc., 1979.

Sartre, Jean Paul. *The Family Idiot: Gustave Flaubert 1821-1857.* Chicago: University of Chicago Press, 1981.

Schiller, Friedrich von. *Letters on the Aesthetic Education of Man.* New York: Routledge, 988.

Steedman, Caroyln. *Strange Dislocations: Childhood and the Idea of Human Interiority, 1780-1930.* London: Virago Press, 1995.

Trilling, Lionel. *Beyond Culture: Essays on Literature and Learning.* New York: The Viking Press, 1965.

—. *The Liberal Imagination: Essays on Literature and Society.* New York: Doubleday Anchor Books, 1957.

Wilner, Joshua. *Feeding on Infinity: Readings in the Romantic Rhetoric of Internalization.* Baltimore; London: Johns Hopkins, 2000.

Wilson, Douglas B. *The Romantic Dream: Wordsworth and the Poetics of the Unconscious.* Lincoln NE; London: University of Nebraska Press, 1993.

Wimsatt, William. "The Structure of Romantic Nature Imagery." *Romanticism and Consciousness: Essays in Criticism.* Ed. Harold Bloom. New York: W.W. Norton, 1970.

Winnocott, D. W. *Playing and Reality.* New York: Basic Books, 1971.

Wordsworth, William. *Lyrical Ballads.* Ed. Michael Mason. New York; London: Longman,1992.

—. *The Prelude: 1799, 1805, 1850.* Ed. Jonathan Wordsworth, M.H. Abrams, and Stephen Gill. New York: Norton, 1979.

—. *The Fenwick Notes of William Wordsworth.* Ed. Jared Curtis. London, Bristol Classical Press, 1993.

—. "Upon Epitaphs" *Prose Works of William Wordsworth.* Ed. William Knight. New York; London: Macmillian, 1896.

Yousef, Nancy. *Isolated Cases: The Anxieties of Autonomy in Enlightenment Philosophy and Romantic Literature.* Ithaca; London: Cornell University Press, 2004.

Chapter Eight

The Founding Father: Benjamin Franklin & His Autobiography

Jeff Morgan, Lynn University

Benjamin Franklin may have had more children than we thought. Reared in a Puritan home, he also came under the influence of the Age of Enlightenment. In the *Autobiography*, these two oppositional forces are reconciled, rendering the author well suited to serve as a model for the young stripling United States struggling in its search for identity. In effect, the founding father moniker so often given to Franklin becomes appropriate in the context of the *Autobiography* because in it Franklin treats all Americans as his offspring who might benefit from filling their minds with his instructive experiences.

At the turn of the nineteenth century, the United States could be seen as needing instruction from a "good parent", as she was still struggling with the transition from a Puritan, agrarian society to one more urban and associated with the Age of Reason. Ormond Seavey writes, "Americans were searching for new models of personal and group identity amid the disruption of behaviour paradigms following the Revolution."[1] The introspective Puritan character looked at the world symbolically in search of some hidden spiritual truth. This belief system was jeopardized by the revelations of scientific truths that explained our world and ourselves. American literature from this period clearly addressed the conflict. In Washington Irving's "Rip Van Winkle," the title character awakens from a twenty-year sleep to a post-revolution America. It appears that an even larger conflict for Rip other than being a deep sleeper is his problem with change. The question arises whether he will be able to adjust and accept the new society. In the end, Rip finds a balance between the two sides thanks to his own simple nature. In "The Legend of Sleepy Hollow," Ichabod Crane exemplifies this duality. He is a man of reason, a teacher,

---

[1] Seavey, *Becoming Benjamin Franklin*, 99.

thrust into the very spiritual, mystical world of Sleepy Hollow. His conflict with these two perspectives will ultimately lead to a climax in which Crane must either fuse these two views or be overwhelmed by one.

Puritan thought dominates the early colonial period of the United States. For the most part, colonists were reared and educated according to strict religious principles. The parenting and educational philosophy of this time can be readily seen in writers such as John Winthrop, Michael Wigglesworth, and Cotton Mather. In "A Model of Christian Charity," a 1630 sermon written and delivered during voyage across the Atlantic, Winthrop preached of the necessity of creating a Christian example both at home and abroad. Similarly, Wigglesworth's very popular "The Day of Doom," a 1662 poem based on the author's dreams, depicted the hell fire awaiting those who did not live the Christian example. In 1710, Cotton Mather's "Essays to Do Good" directly addressed parents, urging them to raise "wise" children deserving of a desirable Christian education so that they may avoid the fires of hell. This was the New England mindset in the late seventeenth and early eighteenth centuries in America. It was very one-sided and was based on truths that existed in faith. The fear of God was the main impetus to learning. Even learning the alphabet was based on Christianity. One learned the alphabet to read the Bible, and one learned the Bible when one learned to read thanks to books like the New England Primer, which taught the letter A through the following rhyme: In *Adam's* Fall/ We Sinned all.

In the light of the likes of Rousseau, it doesn't sound very Romantic to suggest that we are all naturally evil, but the Puritan Era was Romantic in contrast to the Age of Reason that left little room for the imagination and spirituality. After John Clarke introduced John Locke to America in 1730, the floodgates of Reason opened. America's first colleges were founded by religious sects and upon the introduction of Reason, their leaders saw the writing on the wall. In 1754, Thomas Clapp, president of Yale, argued "that colleges without sectarian affiliation would be dangerous educational institutions; they would lack principles to guide them".[2] Reason took a more Scientific approach to existence, explaining things by observation and experiment rather than faith and divine revelation. The lack of spirituality in much of Benjamin Franklin's earlier writings is exemplary. For instance, Franklin begins "Advice to a Young Tradesman, Written by an Old One" in 1748 with "Time is money".[3] A year later in "Proposals Relating to the Education of Youth in Pennsylvania," he argues for the

---

[2] Power, *Educational Philosophy,* 104.
[3] Franklin, *Advice,* 306.

utility in education, emphasizing the need to link education with work, and in "Idea of the English School" from 1751, he presents a methodical look at education geared to help youth ultimately "pass thro' and execute the several offices of civil life".[4]

Paradigm shifts are not new to post-Revolution America. Erik Erikson is quick to point out that all national characters have similar experiences and that "a nation's identity is derived from the ways in which history has, as it were, counterpointed certain opposite potentialities".[5] In the late eighteenth and early nineteenth centuries in America such reconciliation was needed. Writers like Irving alluded to the reconciliation, but Franklin's *Autobiography* paves the way. If we think of the Puritanism of his *Autobiography* as the Romantic side and Reason as the Scientific side, then Normand R. Bernier and Jack E. Williams clearly illustrate the significance of the *Autobiography*. They write that the "absence of Scientism would inhibit constructive collective action, and the removal of Romanticism would result in social atrophy and the obliteration of human creativity." Society needs for the opposites to be reconciled to create a kind of duality, for "without strands from these two ideological antinomies, social systems could not flourish and the humanization of *homo sapiens* would falter".[6] What is needed is entente, and Franklin's *Autobiography*, first published in 1791, has it.

Franklin treats readers as blank slates ready to absorb his teachings. Initially structured in the forme of a letter to his son, the *Autobiography* becomes a parental address to all Americans, advising them how to live their lives. Since imitation was a factor in Franklin's own development, he provides his life as worthy of imitation. After all, Franklin, too, would have believed in Pope's adage that "The proper study of mankind is man." This is at the heart of Franklin's parenting.

It should be no small wonder that the fusion of dual perspectives, the reconciliation of opposites, is at the heart of Franklin's advice to the nation in his *Autobiography* since Franklin himself was reared within the conflict of these opposing views, was able to reconcile them, and shared his path toward reconciliation and the benefits of the reconciliation with a nation eager to come to grips with its own identity. Franklin's father, Josiah, provided the rigid, Puritanical side. A Puritan nonconformist who fled to America in 1683, Josiah tended to focus inward, his library mostly religious works, but his inward focus was not limited to total introspection. Also interested in the conduct of life, he forced his son to

---

[4] Franklin, *Idea,* 108.
[5] Erikson, *Childhood and Society,* 285.
[6] Bernier and Williams, *Beyond Beliefs,* 120.

attend public worship. Edmund Morgan points out that "Josiah originally hoped to see his youngest son in the pulpit".[7] In fact, Josiah's strong morality allowed him to often serve as a judge of right and wrong in the community. P. M. Zall indicates that Franklin's father parented over what he called appearances, but there was an opposing influence in Franklin's life. Granted, Franklin read voraciously texts which touted man's reasoning nature, but many Franklin biographers, like Zall, point to Thomas Denham, who parented Franklin over the business of life.[8] Denham taught Franklin "to keep accounts and to sell goods",[9] and, as H. W. Brands puts it, Denham, "a man who understood success in terms with which Franklin increasingly identified" . . . "instructed him as a father tutored his son".[10]

Franklin's role as a father to the nation has this educational vein. He tries to help his readers live their lives. Molded and shaped by the influences of his readings and experiences but also by Denham and his father, Franklin presents himself as the dual, balanced model for a young America; hence, the *Autobiography* becomes the means by which the blank slates of young Americans can be filled with model behaviour from Franklin's life. To be an effective educator of the public, Franklin must, as Freud argues, show his audience the necessity of controlling their instincts, and to accomplish that, he must create some kind of balance in his presentation. He must discover a "way between the Scylla of non-interference and the Charybdis of frustration. Unless this problem is entirely insoluble, an optimum must be discovered which will enable education to achieve the most and damage the least," and the educator must provide "the right amount of love and yet maintain an effective degree of authority".[11] Franklin accomplished this, in part, by adopting Alexander Pope's adage that man must be taught as if you taught him not. By setting up the *Autobiography* as a letter to his son, he indirectly educates his readers. Moreover, his balance between Puritanism and Reason provides his content with the necessary balance so paramount to successful parenting. Since the young nation itself is experiencing the pulling from both Puritanism and Reason, the balance provided by Franklin helps establish a kind of fusion that will enable the young nation to flower into an Age of Romance in which it experiences its greatest sense of national unity.

---

[7] Morgan, *Benjamin Franklin,* 17.
[8] Zall, *Franklin's Autobiography,* 71.
[9] Van Doren, *Benjamin Franklin,* 70.
[10] Brands, *The First American,* 83.
[11] Freud, *New Introductory Lectures,* 149-150.

Concerning Franklin's spiritual side, he was spiritual but often showed disdain for organized religion. Raised in a Presbyterian household, he writes, "I never was without some religious principles".[12] These principles were primarily Deistic. He believed in an almighty Deity who helps them who help themselves, the immortality of the soul, and the importance of living a virtuous life. However, he felt the divisions of organized religion divided people by sermonizing to them how to be better Presbyterians, for example, as opposed to simply being better humans. Subsequently, Franklin tended to develop his own religious principles, creating his own prayers, and his frequent references to Providence in the *Autobiography* indicate his inclination to believe those prayers could be answered since God's will was a factor in the course of human events and in the felicity of his own life. In fact, for his parents' epitaph, Franklin underscored the role of Providence, urging those who read the stone not to distrust it.

Clearly Franklin's parents did not, for they were both devout Christians who spiritually influenced their son. His father, Josiah, adhered to a Puritan forme of worship rather than switch to the Church of England. His mother, Abiah, came from a family Cotton Mather honourably recognized. The family plan originally was for young Ben to go into the clergy. Furthermore, Franklin's favourite book from the family library was John Bunyan's *The Pilgrim's Progress*. These facts would help explain the significance of Providence in Franklin's life, but they also explain other characteristics. For example, Franklin adopted the Puritan mode of plainness. While making a name for himself in Philadelphia, he dressed plainly, and he and his wife kept a plain house. "We kept no idle servants, our table was plain and simple, our furniture the cheapest. . . my breakfast was a long time bread and milk (no tea), and I ate it out of a twopenny earthen porringer, with a pewter spoon".[13] However, it was the family's books against Deism that ironically steered Franklin to Deism and believing that since God created everything and God is good, everything is good. This type of thinking developed despite youthful experiences such as the wharf building incident in which Franklin defended the goodness and usefulness in stealing some construction stones.

Franklin's Deism evolved into a course of action. To him, felicity rested in his dealing with others. In these actions there must be some kind of utility; actions either help us or not. This belief combined with his belief in Providence helped develop Franklin's character, one which he

---

[12] Franklin, *The Autobiography,* 74.
[13] Ibid., 73.

describes in the *Autobiography* as "tolerable . . . to begin with; I valued it properly, and determined to preserve it".[14] And, not only did he preserve it, but he chose to share the development of his character with a young America so that she might similarly develop. As one moves into Part Three of the *Autobiography*, it becomes clear that Franklin has always been interested in instructing others in the benefits of combining reason and spirituality. He refers in this section to *Poor Richard's Almanac* and how he was able to insert advice for good living into it.

Franklin gives advice for good living throughout the *Autobiography*. He has a penchant for aphoristic phrasing. For example, he suggests that a man is "sometimes more generous when he has but little money than when he has plenty, perhaps through fear of being thought to have but little".[15] Such a statement reveals a bit of Franklin's parenting theory, for, to him, there is reason behind the seemingly unreasonable act of giving money when one has but little of it since it involves a kind of Christian charity that benefits all considered. In this light, Franklin's writing and parenting becomes proverbial. A popular Franklin aphorism from *Poor Richard's Almanac* is mentioned in the *Autobiography*. It goes, "it is hard for an empty sack to stand upright".[16] In this he is able to combine the reason behind making money with the virtuous character the accumulation of wealth can create. It goes well with the previous aphorism since it furthers the reasonableness of acquiring wealth in that it eliminates hesitation in a man's choosing of whether to perform a good act or not, which, to Franklin, was "the most acceptable service of God".[17]

In fact, Franklin thought so highly of man's opportunity to do nothing but good in the world, that he himself undertook a methodical attempt at moral perfection. He developed a systematic approach, turning in his *Autobiography* to aphorism to explain the process he envisioned of mastering thirteen virtues leading to moral perfection.

> And like him who, having a garden to weed, does not attempt to eradicate all the bad herbs at once, which would exceed his reach and his strength, but works on one of the beds at a time, and, having accomplished the first, proceeds to a second, so I should have.[18]

---

[14] Ibid., 52.
[15] Ibid., 23.
[16] Ibid., 89.
[17] Ibid., 74.
[18] Ibid., 78.

This Puritan kind of introspection, inward thinking, and soul searching, was counterbalanced by Franklin's reasonable approach and communicates to those who read his *Autobiography* the benefits of having a similar balance. Moreover, the reason helps the more sermonizing side from becoming dogmatic. In fact, one of the few preachers Franklin liked, a man named Hemphill, had this balance when he spoke from the pulpit. Another preacher he admired, Mr. Whitefield, also had this characteristic, and Franklin went on to reason that Whitefield's particular success also had something to do with his rehearsal of his sermons, leading to yet another instructive point about practice and perfection.

Franklin, of course, never reached that state of perfection, but he continued in the *Autobiography* to combine spirituality with reason to encourage at least the attempt to become a good as one can possibly be. In Part Three, he records his ideas of what a religion ought to try to accomplish. It must start small with a few young single men who will go through Franklin's process of mastering the thirteen virtues. Then, those graduates should reach out to those they deem good candidates for inculcation into a process that ultimately is concerned with creating good citizens more than worshippers of the religion. Franklin's educational or parenting theory has as its base the art of imitation. There are those who imitate Franklin, followed by those who imitate the imitators, ultimately creating a great chain of model behaviour. This notion of self improvement through imitation has always been at the heart of Franklin's own self improvement, clearly evinced in his theories on writing improvement. Furthermore, the notion of sharing that which can benefit others has also been at the heart of Franklin's experience since his early days, and that which is shared does not necessarily need to be in the abstract. Franklin also demonstrates that sharing one's labour, as when he takes his turn at the pump of a leaky ship headed for Boston, can benefit everyone.

Franklin and the others eventually made it to Boston, but the *Autobiography* also contains passages that show that attempts to be good can fail. This in and of itself contributes to the balance of Franklin's educational and parenting theory in that it recognizes and accepts setbacks as unavoidable and prepares the reader and the young nation to deal with them in a manner still exemplary of the combined reasonable and spiritual approach. To illustrate how to respond to mistakes in life, Franklin often refers to the errors he made, such as his breaking into money given to him to hold by a man named Vernon. Franklin was not perfect, but he tried to be, realizing that he would never reach perfection, but knowing that the attempt would improve him. This is very similar to Herman Melville's "seek but do not find" edict in which one must be reasonable in one's goals. Melville's Ahab becomes the Transcendentalist gone mad as his monomania compels him to unreasonably seek a kind of sublime understanding that he feels he can penetrate if he finds and kills Moby-Dick. The properly balanced individual may be better equipped to avoid such excesses, and those who model themselves after Benjamin Franklin model just such a dual character.

To be sure, Franklin grew up with this sense of duality. His early Puritan influences were tempered by his readings of the likes of the religious skeptic Shaftesbury and the realist Collins, both of whom led him from an argumentative character to a more doubting one. Still, he won most of his debates with his brother when he was his apprentice. Furthermore, his successful disputations on religious topics garnered him the label of atheist and infidel. But, above all, the man is balanced. The *Autobiography* opens with Franklin giving reasons why he writes and giving thanks to God for providing a providential hand in his development. So, in conjunction with his Puritan upbringing, Franklin's voracious reading led him to reason, but his reading had another influence.

His reading made him a better writer, and if not for his writing, Franklin doesn't have the opportunity to present his life as a parental role model for the young nation to follow. In fact, modeling becomes the mantra here because it is through modeling that Franklin becomes a good writer, and his readers can now additionally model Franklin's path to success with this very important communication skill. Part Two of the *Autobiography* begins with a letter to Franklin that addresses this very point. Mr. Abel James writes, "The influence writings under that class [autobiography and journal] have on the minds of youth is very great, and has nowhere appeared to me so plain, as in our public friend's journals. It almost insensibly leads youth into the resolution of endeavoring to become as good and eminent as the journalist".[19] The utility of Franklin's writing cannot be clearer, and this model life wouldn't be so well communicated if a young Franklin didn't model other writers, notably Addison and Steele from their *Spectator*. Moreover, so that his tone doesn't become preachy, Franklin uses "iffy" diction to warm the reader to receive advice rather than creating the possibility for contradiction through more absolute diction. Further exemplary from Franklin's writing is his large vocabulary that he, in part, attributes to writing poetry, which demands frequent use of new word choices. Ultimately, in his newspaper,

---

[19] Ibid., 65.

Poor Richard's Almanac, and the *Autobiography*, he achieves success as a model because what he writes is useful and entertaining.

Franklin applies a similar reasonable approach to his health concerns, and a young America could also be well served by modeling aspects of this area. First, Franklin emphasizes the necessity of temperance for "that greater clearness of head and quicker apprehension".[20] In England while young, he worked with men convinced that the drinking of several beers throughout the day contributed to their strength, stamina, and productivity. Ultimately, he was able to reason with them and get them to drink water and eat bread. For economic and character reasons, Franklin stresses a vegetarian diet, and he deems it the more virtuous diet by virtue of the absence of slaughtering life. Still, Franklin is so enamored with reasoning that he uses it to rationalize the eating of fish since big fish eat little fish, suggesting to him that there is no slaughter in him joining the food chain.

Reason is of such a benefit to Franklin's felicity that the *Autobiography* seems to promote its use at every turn. The practice benefits Franklin's love life, enabling him to determine that Miss Read is indeed attracted to him. Reason helps Franklin read people, and Franklin has an aphorism ready for the case. "He that has once done you a kindness will be more ready to do you another than he whom you yourself have obliged".[21] Also, the use of reason benefits in his friendships, creating a bank of friends, a source of mutual utility. This is seen in the Junto, a group formed for mutual improvement, who not only improved themselves through their meetings but their community as well. It is from this group that we benefit from modern libraries and police and fire departments.

Without doubt, Franklin's *Autobiography* serves as a vehicle by which a young America can model a successful man in the hopes of reaching similar success. Nor is it doubtful that reason is a principle means by which that success, whether it constitutes greater wealth or better health, can be obtained. The use of reason is part of a great chain that starts with self-improvement and ends with improving the community. It is important not to forget the role of Franklin's Puritan rearing when mentioning self-improvement, for the inward gaze of the Puritan character is at the core of such activity. Reason, after all, has its limits, as seen in Franklin's classic speckled axe anecdote. In this brief story, a man desires a perfect axe, a metaphor for a perfect character. This then constitutes the Puritan introspective side of Franklin's duality. However, the man discovers that

---

[20] Ibid., 16.
[21] Ibid., 95.

the work required to obtain a perfect axe is excessive, so he settles for a speckled axe, declaring that he actually likes that best. This then exemplifies Franklin's reasonable side, the side that accepts reality, recognizes limitations, and moves on. Such a balance is central to Franklin's character and, in his eye, to the development of the character of America and her citizens. To deftly balance these two sides becomes the theme of the American psyche through the first half of the nineteenth century, and in that respect Franklin's *Autobiography* serves as a text laying the groundwork for American Romanticism by parenting the young nation through the early days after the Revolution. Franklin is in a sense a single parent with a duality within himself that makes him perfectly positioned to be a father to the nation.

Works Cited

Bernier, Normand R. and Jack E. Williams *Beyond Beliefs: Ideological Foundations of American Education*. Englewood Cliffs: Prentice, 1973.

Brands, H. W. *The First American: The Life and Times of Benjamin Franklin*. NewYork: Doubleday, 2000.

Erikson, Erik. *Childhood and Society*. New York: Norton, 1963.

Franklin, Benjamin. "Advice to a Young Tradesman, Written by an Old One." *The Papers of Benjamin Franklin*. Ed. Leonard W. Labaree. New Haven: Yale UP, 1961. 306-308.... *The Autobiography & Other Writings*. Ed. Peter Shaw. New York: Bantam, 1989.... "Idea of the English School." *The Papers of Benjamin Franklin*. Ed Leonard W. Labaree. New Haven: Yale UP, 1961. 102-108.

Freud, Sigmund. "New Introductory Lectures on Psycho-Analysis" *The Standard Edition of the Complete Psychological Works of Sigmund Freud*. Vol. 22. Trans. and Ed. James Strachey. London: Hogarth, 1986. 5-182.

Morgan, Edmund S. *Benjamin Franklin*. New Haven: Yale UP, 2002

Power, Edmund. *Educational Philosophy: A History from the Ancient World to Modern America*. New York: Garland, 1996.

Seavey, Ormond. *Becoming Benjamin Franklin: The Autobiography and the Life*. University Park: Penn St. UP, 1988.

Van Doren, Carl. *Benjamin Franklin*. New York: Bramhall, 1987.

Zall. P. M. *Franklin's Autobiography: A Model Life*. Boston: Twayne, 1989.

Chapter Nine

On Romanticism and Parenting in Practise

Sarah Moss,
University of Kent at Canterbury

I used to work on Romanticism and travel, and specifically on Romantic responses to and interpretations of the great white spaces of the Far North. I used to get travel grants to go there myself, and I used to take a big plane and then a little plane and then a bus in a place where I didn't speak the language and couldn't even read the road signs, carrying a small backpack containing a notebook and pen, a bit of Wordsworth and a change of clothes. I used to go for long walks on my own or with a like-minded friend, trading quotes and in-jokes and rumours about tenure-track jobs as we crossed the Peak District on ancient pathways or quietly abandoned a conference for an afternoon. We planned the EGO (English Graduates in Oxford) hit squad, a small terrorist organisation which would take out dead wood in desirable English departments to produce vacancies lower down the pay-scales. We were surprised but pleased when a fellow graduate student announced her pregnancy. She was an excellent scholar and teacher so it meant less competition for jobs.

Then it happened to me. I was finishing the Arctic book by then. I went on applying for travel grants for the first few weeks, until it hit me that I was so tired I was waking to find I'd gone to sleep in the Bodleian Library with my head on my laptop, generating a screen full of nonsense even greater than I'd have produced if I'd stayed awake, and so sick I had to get off my bike and throw up in the gutter on my way to work. After I'd let down some friends and colleagues by insisting I could and would meet editorial deadlines, take transatlantic flights, give papers I hadn't yet written, I began to get the message. My growing bump became known to me and my aforementioned like-minded friend as the fetal hijacker (as his pram was later to be The Enemy, short for the pram in the hall that is the enemy of promise). I had been hijacked. The practise of Romanticism was not compatible with the practise of parenting. I didn't even feel safe climbing the library ladders to reach the Cornell Wordsworth, stored ten feet up by a mullioned window looking across Radcliffe Square to All Souls. Exiled from the dreaming spires to the antenatal clinic, I finished the Arctic book and made a half-hearted start on my next project, a study of food and gender in Romantic-era women's fiction, but in the afternoons I went home – walking, now, my centre of gravity too high for the bike, and binged secretly on pregnancy handbooks, reading and re-reading their strictures and reassurances with a devotion that could very usefully have been applied to the works of Habermas or Kristeva or any of the other major thinkers with whom one tends to claim a greater acquaintance than the circumstances entirely justify. Sometimes, ashamed to spend money on such a conspicuously ephemeral genre, I slipped quietly down the stairs at the back of the local history section in Blackwells, into the fabled Norrington Room which runs under the gardens of Trinity College and houses more books than even I have ever seen assembled in one place anywhere else. In a corner between anthropological theory and political science is popular medicine, and at the bottom of the shelf, handily located where the heavily pregnant can reach, is a luscious spread of pregnancy handbooks. I didn't know any political scientists and my only anthropologist friend was in Amsterdam, so I could crouch there until the fear of deep vein thrombosis (or placental abruption or fetal malposition or whatever else was fear of the day) sent me scurrying in shame-faced search of the latest offerings from Studies in Romanticism. I have always known that if only I would concentrate properly on research, my troubles would turn out to be imaginary, the deluded product of an undisciplined mind, and pregnancy was no exception, except that I couldn't muster the discipline. A bit like Coleridge and opium, really, between bouts of hopeless self-indulgence I made ambitious schedules of works I would complete as soon as I'd pulled myself together. At seven months I was signed off sick with stress-related illness, the stress partly generated by my appalled recognition that whatever Wordsworth had to say about it, poetry and parenting have about as much in common as airborne combat and a persistent vegetative state (and we all know which is which).

After the hijacker was born, it took me two years to feel I had recovered full intellectual function (it also took him two years adopt the general consensus about the division of time into day and night, which may have had something to do with my intellectual dysfunction). I kept working on the food and gender project, the addiction to pregnancy handbooks now replaced by a compulsion for birth stories born of gnawing regret about the highly medicalised hospital birth I'd ended up having. In due course I began to work on Wollstonecraft, who has enormously complicated attitudes to food and femininity about which you can read elsewhere (see Sarah Moss, *Sweet Surrender: Food and Gender in British Women's Fiction 1774 – 1837*, Manchester University Press, forthcoming 2008 babies permitting).

Wollstonecraft's most consistent view, I think, is that women's consumption is justified only by their productions, that it is in the nature of femininity, and not of masculinity, that we have no a priori entitlement to consume. There is a sense that women betray themselves by consuming (the old story) but also a more radical demand that we redeem ourselves by producing. It is not hard to contextualise this in relation to recent – well, fairly recent, before the birth of my second child – scholarship on women in the eighteenth century literary marketplace,[1] but I saw, in the light of my own current experiences as a pregnant Romanticist, that the late eighteenth century also has very particular views about the relationship between women's consumption and reproduction. Food goes in and babies (as well as books) come out. There is, so far as I can see, an absolutely transhistorical tendency to invert this relationship, so that it is not that women's eating enables our production, which would suggest that women should eat well and often, but that production justifies or even excuses consumption, that our cultural entitlement to food depends entirely on the satisfactory production of babies (or possibly books, or failing that, other goods and services according to class, education and historical period). Wollstonecraft is startlingly explicit about this: women who do not produce, may not consume:

> Men are certainly more under the influence of their appetites than women; and their appetites are more depraved by unbridled indulgence and the fastidious contrivances of satiety. Luxury has introduced a refinement in eating, which destroys the constitution; and, a degree of gluttony which is so beastly, that a perception of seemliness of behaviour must be worn out before one being could eat immoderately in the presence of another, and afterwards complain of the oppression that his intemperance naturally produced. Some women, particularly French women, have also lost a sense of decency in this respect; for they will talk very calmly of an indigestion. It were to be wished that idleness was not allowed to generate, on the rank soil of wealth, those swarms of summer insects that feed on putrefaction, we should not then be disgusted by the sight of such brutal excesses.[2]

---

[1] See Moss.
[2] *Vindication*, 207.

The connection between idleness and over-eating here is interesting, and Wollstonecraft's disgust seems excessive (there is no suggestion that the 'summer insects' eat in a revolting manner, but only that there is something self-evidently repellent about the female appetite). It is the combination of such women's insistence on consuming and refusal to produce that gives rise to such horror, and this is bourn out by Wollstonecraft's writing about pregnancy, birth and breastfeeding. In the opening pages of Mary, the heroine's mother Eliza, "was educated with the expectation of a large fortune, of course became a mere machine." "As she was sometimes obliged to be alone, or only with her French waiting-maid" she "sends to the metropolis" for "those most delightful substitutes for bodily dissipation, novels." She has "two most beautiful dogs", of which she is extremely fond, but her fondness "proceeded from vanity, it gave her an opportunity of lisping out the prettiest French expressions of ecstatic fondness, in accents that had never been attuned by tenderness." Needless to say, Eliza is not a good mother, and in fact dies a well-deserved death from laziness in childbirth and her refusal to breastfeed:

> In due time she brought forth a son, a feeble babe; and the following year a daughter. After the mother's throes she felt very few sentiments of maternal tenderness; the children were given to nurses, and she played with her dogs. Want of exercise prevented the least chance of her recovering strength; and two or three milk fevers brought on a consumption, to which her constitution tended. Her children all died in their infancy, except the two first, and she began to grow fond of the son, as he was remarkably handsome. For years she divided her time between the sofa, and the card-table. She thought not of death, though on the borders of the grave; nor did any of the duties of her station occur to her as necessary.[3]

This laconic summary of the effects of refusing post-natal exercise is almost funny in its brevity – there is certainly no attempt to characterise Eliza except in terms of what she produces and consumes – but again, gluttony (this time displaced into reading, a very common eighteenth century analogy) is matched by incompetence in the production of babies and milk. Eliza deserves to die because she is a net drain on resources, an extreme position even by Wollstonecraft's frequently startling standards.

The difficulty of justifying consumption by production is, of course, that consumption necessarily takes place first, and this might be a useful

---

[3] *Mary* and *Maria*/ Mary Shelley, *Matilda*, 7.

place to locate a nexus of anxiety surrounding pregnancy and food, and also pregnancy and work. I found my first pregnancy so difficult partly because I hadn't justified all the time off and broken deadlines and unattended conferences. I was taking what I hadn't earned, and the pregnancy books were telling me that if I didn't take it I wouldn't earn it, that sick pregnant women must rest and not work and not take transatlantic flights and not stay up late at night trying to get served at the bar with drinks for visiting senior Romanticists who might one day influence a job or a book or a research grant on pain of losing or damaging the baby, whose successful gestation is the only excuse for behaving like that in the first place. I can see now that it is horribly circular, and that the stress and anxiety which exacerbated my pre-eclampsia and cardiac problems were legitimate currents running through my double indenture to academia and maternity, rival forms of production which cancelled out my permission to consume. It was following Wollstonecraft's reviews of Romantic-era pregnancy and breastfeeding handbooks and putting together late eighteenth century discussions of pregnancy and breast-feeding with more obvious discourses on gender and print culture which brought me to this realisation. Wollstonecraft, of course, is no more writing in a discursive vacuum than I am now, and the anxiety – then and now – about pregnant women's eating is widespread.

The first advice offered to any British or North American woman planning a pregnancy now is about diet. Eat for a healthy baby. There is an explicit view that what you put in is what you get out – put the right food into a woman's body and the right baby will appear. No peanuts (or your baby will have allergies). No soft cheese, cured meat, shellfish, raw or partially cooked eggs, rare beef, bagged salads, pate, liver, cold pies, quiches or pastries (or you'll get food poisoning and miscarry). No alcohol or the baby will have Foetal Alcohol Syndrome (and no, there is no safe amount. Put that liqueur chocolate back.) And, to quote from a National Health Service booklet issued to all pregnant women in the UK, 'Sorry, girls, but pregnancy isn't a licence to eat cakes, quite the reverse! It's more important than ever to eat a healthy balanced diet now you've got another life to think about.' (Emma's Diary, p.12). The discourse is viciously infantilizing, as if there is a relationship between the society represented by these writers and the baby which has only the most casual bearing on the pregnant woman (or 'mum-to-be', as if one's identity is in waiting). There is an obvious fear that women, by indulging themselves, will damage their babies, consuming not to produce but for personal gratification. Dietary proscription and prescription focus exclusively on the baby's needs: 'Eat well washed raw vegetables as cooking destroys many of the nutrients'; 'Milk is a good source of calcium needed for bones and teeth'; 'keep up your intake of essential fatty acids...which are important for your baby's brain and eyesight.' (Emma's Diary p.12). There is palpable anxiety about the possibility of consumption in excess of what is required to produce: 'You don't actually need to eat more until the last trimester when your overall calorie needs increase...cut out 'empty' junk foods, which have no nutritional value...stay away from sugary cereals.' In other words, pregnancy gives you permission to eat only the ingredients required to make a good baby.

I didn't notice this until I was reading Romantic-era pregnancy advice literature with my critical faculties switched on. William Buchan, best-selling celebrity obstetrician of the late eighteenth century, admiringly reviewed by Wollstonecraft, writes:

> In laying down rules of temperance, I do not wish to impose any restraint on the moderate use of good and wholesome food or drink: but under these heads we must not include spirituous liquors; relaxing and often-repeated draughts of hot coffee and tea; salted, smoke-dried, and highly-seasoned meats; salt fish; rich gravies; heavy sauces; almost indigestible pastry; and sour unripe fruits, of which women in general are immoderately fond. We pity the green-sick girl, whose longing for such trash is one of the causes as well as one of the effects of her disease; but can any woman, capable of the least reflection, continue to gratify a perverse appetite by the use of the most pernicious crudities? p13

Alexander Hamilton goes even further, arguing that the phenomenon of pregnancy cravings is invented by pregnant women and the midwives who have traditionally cared for them as part of a female conspiracy to legitimise women's innate gluttony and manipulate husbands into providing expensive delicacies to which women would not usually have access. He advises that, "Women often claim indulgence in their longings, by an argument which is well calculated to ensure success, the dangers which might happen to the child from their cravings being neglected."[4]

As with the NHS booklet, these are only a particularly concise example of a large chorus of voices carolling the same interdictions (and you will have to take this on trust because there is no way I can take a breastfeeding baby with me to the British Library to find more examples to cite. I read them for the book, between babies.) Don't eat the foods of which women in general are immodestly fond, be it cake, chocolate or fruit, and do, in moderation, eat what the writers decree to be good and

---

[4] Hamilton, *Management of Female Complaints*, 190.

wholesome. Your appetite is for garbage ('junk' in modern parlance, 'trash' for Buchan) and the implication is that if you gratify this desire for refuse your baby will be rubbish. The level of misogyny here startles me as I uncover it, and I have a final observation before I go back to my baby: the foods proscribed by both Buchan and the National Health Service are those associated with high status and masculinity. Most of Buchan's list – the 'highly-seasoned meats', 'rich gravies' and 'heavy sauces' are associated with French cuisine, which achieved its high status in England during this period (later pregnancy books make explicit their concern that it is necessary to eat English food to produce English subjects). The pate, cured meats, soft and unpasteurised cheeses which are forbidden to modern British women are also usually from mainland Europe and more specifically associated with France, while most of the other forbidden foods are expensive and typically consumed by the upper classes. Pregnant women, in other words, are commanded to abjure status. Don't, in the twenty-first century, fly to conferences, stay up late working, push to get served at the bar. "You're pregnant now," as several health professionals rather redundantly admonished me. And don't, in the romantic era, stay out late dancing, attend crowded public events, or travel to see friends (although, interestingly, travelling to make sure the baby is born in the country and not in London is strongly recommended). The price of maternity seems to change little in 250 years.

I have written most of this piece, a few sentences at a time, with my second baby asleep on my chest. He doesn't like to nap in his crib, and when he was newborn it was easy enough to lean back on the sofa so he didn't slide down while I sat with my laptop on my lap and reached past him to the keyboard. He's five months old now and his feet rest dangerously near the keyboard. One little wriggle towards the touchpad and I could lose a lot of work. But I keep doing it, partly because letting him sleep in my arms assuages some tiny proportion of the storms of guilt over my imminent return to work, partly because it's not worth letting him cry in his crib for half an hour for the sake of a twenty minute nap, but also, I think, because it feels salutary, this literal balancing act. Soon I'll be able to go the British Library again and write pieces with full references and proper footnotes again, some part of my mind always resting over my children as I fly to conferences and buy drinks for senior colleagues and meet deadlines, but for now this is it, my postcard from that liminal place where the practise of Romanticism and the practise of parenting happen together. This is what I do now (he's shifting on my shoulder, about to wake up and look around gravely at the coloured lights and clicking buttons that command so much of Mummy's attention) and I would not have it otherwise.

Works Cited

Hamilton, Alexander. *A Treatise on the Management of Female Complaints and of Children in Early Infancy.* London, 1781.

Moss, Sarah. 'Spilling the Beans: Eating and Authorship in Frances Burney's Early Journals', *Women's Writing.* 13.3 (Oct 2006).

Wollstonecraft, Mary. *Mary* and *Maria/* Mary Shelley, *Matilda.* Ed. Janet Todd. London: Penguin, 1991.

—. *Vindication of the Rights of Woman.* Ed. Janet Todd. Harmondsworth: Penguin, 1997.

Contributors

CATHERINE E. ANDERSON
Catherine E. Anderson is a Ph.D. candidate in the History of Art and Architecture at Brown University. Her dissertation examines the representation of race and the politics of imperial identity in late Victorian painting. She received her A.B. and M.A. in Art History from the University of California at Davis.

INGRID BROSZEIT-RIEGER
Ingrid Broszeit-Rieger is Associate Professor of German at Oakland University in Rochester, Michigan. She received the equivalent of a Master's degree in English, German, and Education from the University of Münster, Germany, in 1988, and a Ph.D. in German from the University of Virginia in 2001. She continues to publish on Goethe, most recently "Transgressions of Gender and Generation in the Families of Goethe's *Meister*" forthcoming in Jeffrey Cass and Larry Peer, eds., *Romantic Border Crossings* with Ashgate Press. Her current project addresses family systems and feminine identity formation in Goethe's novels.

ROBERT C. HALE
Robert C. Hale serves as an Associate Professor of English at Monmouth College, in Monmouth, Illinois where he teaches courses in nineteenth- and twentieth-century British literature. Along with Wordsworth and representations of mothers, his scholarly interests include psychoanalytic approaches to literature, Romantic poetry, and Victorian painting and poetry. Rob also holds the esteemed position of *Dad* to daughter, Barbara, and son, Eddie.

BRIAN HOLLINGWORTH
Brian Hollingworth was most recently the Head of English at the University of Derby; he previously taught at the University of Leeds after being the Head of English at Methodist College in Hong Kong. He received his M.A. from Manchester University and his Ph.D. from Nottingham. His publications include *Songs of the People, Lancashire Dialect Poetry of the Industrial Revolution* (Manchester, 1977) and *Maria Edgeworth's Irish Writing: Language, History, Politics* (Macmillan, 1997).

JEFF MORGAN
Jeff Morgan chairs the English Department at Lynn University in Boca Raton, Florida. He is the author of *Sarah Orne Jewett's Feminine Pastoral Vision: The Country of the Pointed Firs*, and the editor of a new edition of Jewett's *Country*, providing notes and a bibliography. His essay "Deconstructing Paradise: Elizabeth Stuart Phelps's *The Story of Avis*" appeared in *Florida English,* and his poetry has appeared in numerous publications. He earned his Ph.D. in English from Case Western Reserve University, his M.A. in English from Pan American University, and his B.A. in English from Ohio University. He lives in Boynton Beach, Florida with his wife, Dana, and their son, Colin.

SARAH MOSS
Sarah Moss has a B.A., M.St. and D.Phil. from Oxford University, where she also spent three years as a Junior Research Fellow. She is now Lecturer in English Literature at the University of Kent, and her second book *Sweet Surrender: Food and Gender in British Women's Fiction 1774 – 1837*, will be appearing with Manchester University Press in 2008.

AMY CAROL REEVES
Amy Carol Reeves holds her Ph.D. in nineteenth-century British literature from the University of South Carolina. Her dissertation examined the politics of children's literature by British women writers in the Romantic era. She recently published an article for *The Victorian Newsletter* entitled "Emily Brontë's Pedagogy of Desire in *Wuthering Heights*."

DAVID B. RUDERMAN

David B. Ruderman is a Ph.D. candidate in English Language and Literature at the University of Michigan. His dissertation project is entitled *'Stranger-wise': Infancy and Aesthetics in 19th-century British Poetry and Poetics*. Also a poet and musician, he lives in Ann Arbor Michigan with his two young children.

CAROLYN A. WEBER

Carolyn A. Weber is an assistant professor at Seattle University in Seattle, Washington. She received her B.A. Hon. from the University of Western Ontario in London, Canada and her M.Phil. and D.Phil. from Oxford University, England. Her research interests and publications include theories and portrayals of the soul in Romantic literature, women's writing, and family dynamics (particularly within the Shelley circle). She is currently at work on a collection on the Female Gothic. She resides in Seattle with her husband, Kent, and their daughter, Victoria Kelly.